THE SECRETS OF
ASTROLOGY

A complete guide to Sun signs, planets, houses, and more

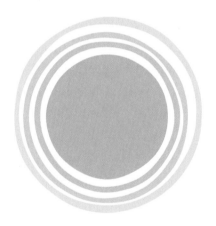

THE SECRETS OF
ASTROLOGY

A complete guide to Sun signs, planets, houses, and more

DK | Penguin Random House

US Editor **Margaret Parrish**
Project Editor **Radhika Haswani**
Consultant **Kim Farley**
Art Editors **Alison Shackleton,**
Brandie Tully-Scott
Jacket Designer **Steven Marsden**
Jacket Coordinator **Issy Walsh**
DTP Designer **Sachin Gupta**
Pre-production Producer **Heather Blagden**
Senior Producer **Igrain Roberts**
Publishing Manager **Francesca Young**
Publishing Director **Sarah Larter**

Illustrated by **Keith Hagan**

This adapted and abridged version's content
previously published in *Astrology*
by Carole Taylor.

This American Edition, 2021
First American Edition, 2018
Published in the United States by DK Publishing
1450 Broadway, Suite 801, New York, NY 10018

Published in Great Britain by Dorling Kindersley Limited

A catalog record for this book is available from
the Library of Congress.
ISBN 978-0-7440-5975-5

DK books are available at special discounts when purchased
in bulk for sales promotions, premiums, fund-raising, or
educational use. For details, contact: DK Publishing Special
Markets, 1450 Broadway, Suite 801, New York, NY 10018
SpecialSales@dk.com

Printed and bound in China

For the curious
www.dk.com

MIX
Paper from
responsible sources
FSC™ C018179

This book was made with Forest
Stewardship Council™ certified paper—
one small step in DK's commitment to a
sustainable future. For more information
go to www.dk.com/our-green-pledge

CONTENTS

THE **ZODIAC SIGNS** **24**

THE **PLANETS**   **84**

♊ ♋ ♌ ♍ ♎ ♏ ♐ ♑ ♒ ♓ ♈ ♉

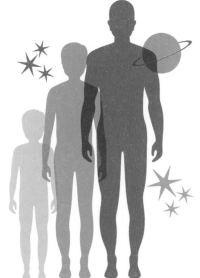

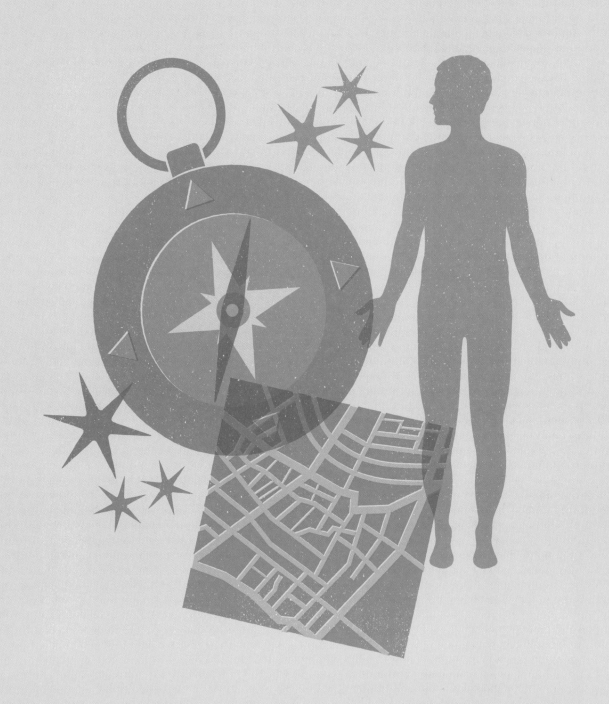

"... THE CHART IS A KIND OF TREASURE MAP, AND THE REAL SEARCH IS AN INTERNAL ONE."

Kim Farley, Journey Through Astrology:
Charting the Astrological Voyage of Discovery

THE **STORY** OF **ASTROLOGY**

WHAT IS ASTROLOGY?

Astrology is all about studying the movements and patterns of the planets, stars, and other elements in space and showing how they affect who we are and how we behave.

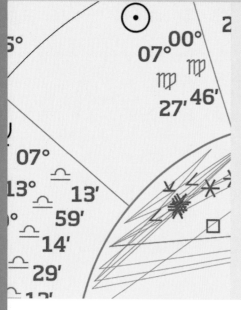

How astrology began

The kind of astrology practiced today began in the ancient world of Babylon and Greece. The Babylonians created the concept of the zodiac (the 12 animal constellations) and the practice of finding meaning in the movements of the planets. The Greeks took up these ideas after the conquests of Alexander the Great in the 4th century BCE. Shaped by their own beliefs about the stars and heavens, they created the "horoscope" we know today.

What is a horoscope?

A horoscope is a wheel-shaped picture of the heavens at a particular time and place, with the person looking at it in the center. The 12 zodiac signs are at the edge of the horoscope wheel, and the Sun, Moon, and the planets are arranged

"" Your **birth chart** is an **image of you** and how you fit into the world. ""

around the wheel according to their position in the sky.

Your birth chart

Your horoscope is also called your birth chart. It is an image of you and how you fit into the world. Its symbols describe your unique personality and how this guides your feelings and behavior. It shows what is important to you and how you can find ways to shine.

IN THE BEGINNING

Astrology has existed since ancient times. It began in Mesopotamia (the modern-day Middle East) and spread to Europe, then worldwide. It has had highs and lows of popularity. Today, as in the past, people use it to help them live their best lives.

Starting in Babylonia

Humans have always looked to the skies to answer questions about religion, farming, and the passage of time. Lunar cycles, for instance, were recorded as long as 25,000 years ago. Babylonian astronomers were the first to document the cycle of the planets. From them, we get the 12 signs of the zodiac, which track the Sun's movement through the constellations. By charting how and when the planets move, ancient astronomers could make predictions about the future.

To Greece and Rome

Astrology next spread to Greece and Egypt, where the horoscope was born. It combined the zodiac, Greek ideas of the four elements and heavenly bodies, and Egyptian

> " It seems a natural part of human experience to **seek meaning in the sky**. "

symbolism. In ancient Rome, everyone–from emperors to common people–looked to astrology for answers.

A high point
The Medieval and Renaissance periods in Europe were a high point in astrology's history. It was often classed as one of the liberal arts at universities, and it formed the basis of some medical practices.

Most royal courts had an astrologer-astronomer in residence. At the same time, the Renaissance brought a new search for scientific knowledge, and astrology's popularity declined.

Astrology now
At the end of the 19th century, people began to believe that there was a link between astrology and psychology.

Astrologers also saw that our universe happens both outside and within us and that the two realms are linked. Today, people are again turning to astrology. As in ancient times, it shows us how we can live our best lives in rhythm with the heavenly pattern.

ASTROLOGY **TODAY**

The full zodiac is far more complex than the simple "Sun-sign" horoscopes in newspapers. Modern astrology combines psychology and astrology. It offers answers to who we are and why we act as we do.

Popular horoscope

In 1930, British astrologer R. H. Naylor wrote a newspaper article about the horoscope of the newborn princess, Margaret. The article was popular, and he was hired to write more. When he correctly predicted an air disaster, he was given a weekly column. Other British papers soon had similar horoscope columns.

Naylor invented a system based on the 12 zodiac signs. He placed (in order) each sign in the first astrological house, noting where the planets fell on the wheel. For a person born with the Sun in Aries, the sign of Aries would be in the 1st house, and so on, around the wheel. With this system, he could create 12 short forecasts based on the date of a person's birth.

> " Older **forms** of astrology have been renewed for **today's audience**. "

Professional astrologers often think Sun-sign columns are too simplistic. But without them, most people would never have heard of astrology.

Modern changes

The most significant development in modern astrology has been the incorporation of psychology into the field. This is known as psychological astrology.

Psychology provides what astrology naturally lacks– a theory of why people behave the way they do and how our personalities are formed.

Astrology now

Today, astrology is enjoying a surge in popularity. Curiosity now stretches beyond Sun signs to include the whole birth chart.

Uncertainty about the future pushes many to seek wisdom from spiritual traditions. Interest in mysticism is not just found in the pull toward astrology, but also in literature, fashion, film, and other areas. Astrology is a practical tool that can be applied to all areas of life. It also speaks to our need for a spiritual connection, a counter to the rationalism of modern science.

ASTROLOGY AND **ME**

Astrology is an imaginative yet practical art. It applies to all aspects of life and connects our inner self to the outer world. The better we know ourselves, the more harmonious and productive our lives can be.

A guide for life

Most of the time, life may run smoothly. In a crisis, however, it is useful to have a tool that lets you see what is happening at a deeper level. Psychology and astrology speak to this inner meaning. Astrology encourages you to reflect on who you are and why you have certain personality traits. It helps you understand others, too. Astrology can also show you practical ways forward. For example, if Saturn is active in your chart, this is probably not a good time to branch out; instead, it may be better for you to focus your energies. On the other hand, if Uranus is active, you may want to assert yourself.

Cycles and change

Nothing we do occurs in a vacuum—our actions are set

" **Forecasting** lets you glimpse the future. It shows you **which path** might be the **most fruitful** to take. "

within the context of our lives and shaped by our needs and desires. Life always has phases and cycles and an underlying sense of growth and development. The one constant in the universe is change, and we are all subject to it. Astrology sees this in terms of planetary cycles–the planets circuiting the chart and marking the chapters of our lives.

Inner and exterior life
The birth chart shows both inner and outer circumstances, and it makes a link between the two. It shows how you can change your outer situation by understanding your inner psychology. Personal understanding and growth are important in astrology. You should not just react to life, but live it fully as your best self. Astrology helps you do this.

How to use astrology
Natal (or birth) astrology is most useful in helping to reveal your character and identify your skills, potentials, and motivations. Forecasting then lets you glimpse into the future–not telling you what will happen, but showing you the path that might be the most fruitful for you to take.

♉ ♊ ♋ ♌ ♍ ♎ ♏ ♐ ♑ ♒ ♓ ♈

THINK LIKE AN
ASTROLOGER

Astrology belongs to a magical mindset that sees Earth as a reflection of the heavens. You do not have to be a philosopher to use astrology, but it does help your understanding of it.

As above, so below

Astrology rests on an ancient philosophy: "As above, so below." This means that life on Earth is a mirror of the heavenly picture.

Each planet governs everything in the universe that reflects its particular energy. So, the Sun governs solar things (monarchs, leaders, gold, sunflowers, the heart). The Moon governs lunar things (mothers and carers, food and nourishment). Each planet has a territory that reaches through every level of life, from the physical to the mental.

It's all in us

The ancient worldview was that "man is a microcosm," which means that each of us is a universe in miniature. Your birth chart reflects this view.

♊ ♋ ♌ ♍ ♎ ♏ ♐ ♑ ♒ ♓ ♈ ♉

> " To **appreciate** and work with **astrology**, you need to **suspend a conventional way of thinking**. "

Earth-centered

Astrology does not fit into a scientific worldview. It is an Earth-centered view that gives us a poetic vision of life. The birth chart is a magical space where "rational" thinking gives way to a symbolic mindset. To work with astrology, it is necessary to suspend conventional thinking and embrace ancient ideas of the universe.

The nature of symbols

In astrology, we must learn how to interpret symbols. A symbol does not offer a one-size-fits-all description. For example, Venus is our drive to create relationships, but it also describes our sense of beauty, our artistic potential, and how we dress and groom ourselves.

Each time we read a chart, we have to think symbolically and use our imaginations to interpret the chart because each symbol is lived at many levels. This makes it impossible for a natal chart to tell us exactly what we should do. If it did make such exact predictions, it would suggest that our lives are fated. Instead, the chart reveals the rich and beautiful pattern of our individual lives.

ZODIAC SIGNS, PLANETS, AND MORE

Astrology is based on the birth chart, which contains the planets, signs, houses, and more. Together, they make up the map of a person.

YOUR SUN SIGN

We say "She's a Scorpio" or "He's a Gemini" as shorthand for the zodiac sign occupied by the Sun when a person was born. The Sun is the center of a birth chart. It holds a person's creative gift and sense of identity.

The Sun
see pp.88–91

YOUR INDIVIDUAL MAP

Most people know their "Sun sign," but we are all much more than one sign.

The horoscope (birth or natal chart) is a stylized map of the heavens at the time and place of your birth. It reflects you and what motivates you. It says something about the circumstances of your life and what you hope to achieve. It combines past experiences, present situations, and future possibilities.

Your Birth Chart see pp.166–183

YOUR MOON SIGN

The Moon represents our basic needs, instincts, and emotional lives. As the brightest beings in the sky, the Sun and Moon are called the "Luminaries." They are the central forces in any chart.

The Moon see pp.92–95

"The Sun represents a person's individual creative gift and sense of identity."

YOUR PLANETS

The Sun is at the center of both the solar system and the zodiac. Each planets represents a basic human drive. For instance, Mercury shows our need to communicate and learn, while Mars is our impulse to fight and compete.

The Planets see pp.84–135

YOUR HOUSES

A birth chart is divided into 12 houses, covering every area of life. Each planet resides in a house. A planet expresses itself according to the zodiac sign it occupies and its house.

The Houses see pp.136–165

YOUR ZODIAC SIGNS

In a chart, each planet occupies a sign of the zodiac. A person may have the Sun in Scorpio, the Moon in Taurus, Mercury in Sagittarius, and so on…. Together, they create a unique birth chart.

The Zodiac Signs see pp.24–83

YOUR ASCENDANT OR RISING SIGN

Your Ascendant is the zodiac sign that was rising on the eastern horizon when you were born. It is one of the four "angles" that divide the chart in quarters. The Ascendant is precise; it represents your birth at a very particular moment.

YOUR ANGLES

Each chart has two axes. The first is the Ascendant-Descendant. It shows the line of the horizon, linking east to west. The Ascendant symbolizes birth and new beginnings.

The Descendant lies opposite and shows our "other half." The second axis is the MC-IC. MC stands for "Medium Coeli" (Latin for "middle of the heavens"). IC is "Imum Coeli" ("bottom of the heavens").

These points divide the chart south to north. The MC gives information about ambitions, career, and achievements. The IC represents home, family, and your inner world.

THE
ZODIAC SIGNS

THE WHEEL OF LIFE

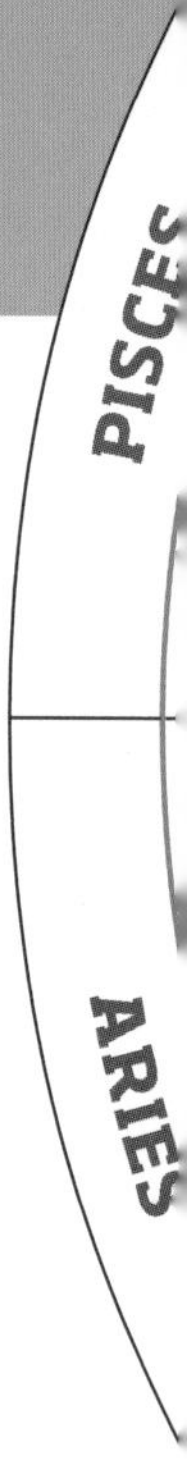

The zodiac is the foundation of astrology. Divided into 12 zodiac signs that follow the seasonal year, it forms the bounding wheel of the birth chart.

The circle of life

The zodiac represents one full circuit of the Sun. The spring equinox starts the year. Here, the Sun enters the bold sign of Aries. The year ends with the journey in Pisces, whose nature is to release. Each sign builds on the story.

The signs in your chart

A **planet** represents a particular human drive. For example, the Moon is our basic need for food and safety.

A **sign** represents the way something in the chart shows itself. The way your planets and other chart factors express themselves depends on the sign they occupy.

Your **Sun sign** is the sign occupied by the Sun on the day you were born. This zodiac sign forms the core of your life experiences–the qualities and talents you are now developing.

All your planets occupy a **zodiac sign**. Every chart contains all 12 signs. Each sign will have an influence somewhere in your life.

PISCES

ARIES

"

Your **Sun sign** symbolizes your most **essential creative gift**.

"

AQUARIUS

THE WATER BEARER

JANUARY 20–FEBRUARY 18

CAPRICORN

THE GOAT

DECEMBER 22–JANUARY 19

SAGITTARIUS

THE ARCHER

NOVEMBER 22–DECEMBER 21

SCORPIO

THE SCORPION

OCTOBER 23–NOVEMBER 21

LIBRA

THE SCALES

SEPTEMBER 23–OCTOBER 22

THE FISHES

FEBRUARY 19–MARCH 20

THE RAM

MARCH 21–APRIL 20

THE VIRGIN

AUGUST 23–SEPTEMBER 22

VIRGO

THE BULL

APRIL 21–MAY 21

THE TWINS

MAY 22–JUNE 21

THE CRAB

JUNE 22–JULY 22

THE LION

JULY 23–AUGUST 22

LEO

TAURUS

GEMINI

CANCER

POLARITY, ELEMENTS, AND **MODES**.

The 12 signs are grouped into two polarities, four elements, and three modes. Their balance in your chart gives powerful information about who you are.

The two polarities

 The positive signs have an extroverted and upbeat quality. They need activity and people time.

 The negative signs are more introverted and low-key. They focus on the interior world and personal experience.

The four elements

 Fire is bold and dramatic, giving off heat and energy. Planets in fire are courageous, with a sense of purpose.

Earth is solid and real. Planets here are grounded, practical, and unsentimental.

Air is home to ideas and thoughts. Planets in air express themselves verbally. They are rational and curious about life.

 Water in nature can be cleansing, raging, or vast, like the ocean. Planets in water act with strong feelings and intuition.

The three modes

 The cardinal signs begin the four seasons of the year. Planets in these signs take initiative. Cardinal makes the first move and needs action.

 The fixed signs reflect the middle of each season, when the weather is settled. Planets in fixed signs are steadfast, stable, and persistent.

 The mutable signs mark the end of the seasons and are known for change and adaptability.

PISCES

ARIES

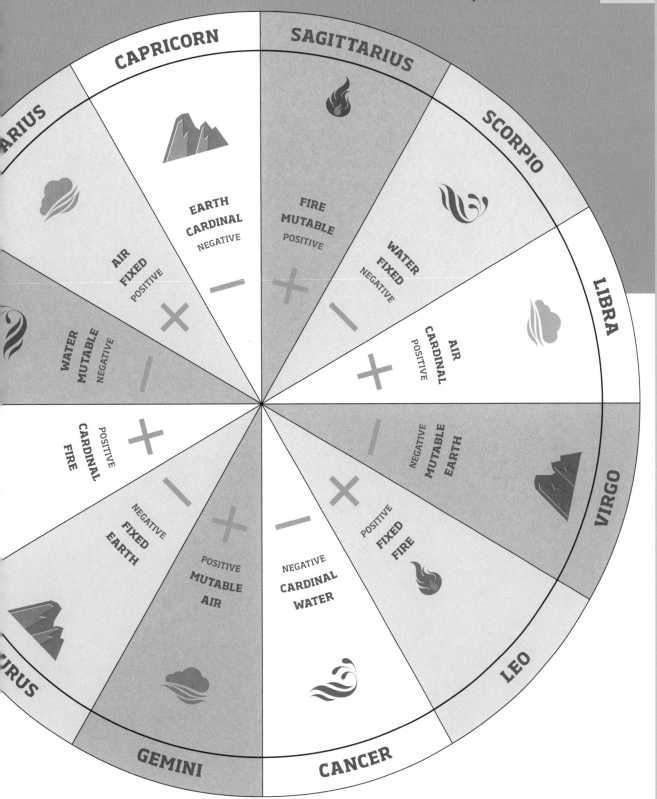

Exploring your chart

Find the balance in your chart by noting the signs occupied by your Sun, Moon, Mercury, Venus, Mars, Jupiter, and Saturn. Also look for the sign where your Ascendant falls.

When a polarity, element, or mode is strongly represented, you will express it easily. For an element or mode, this means having at least two planets there. If you don't have any planets in this area, it might be hard for you to show these qualities.

If you have just one planet in a polarity, element, or mode, you will express it through that planet only, often forcefully.

THE ELEMENTS IN YOUR CHART
ELEMENT HIGH

FIRE
You tend to be self-motivated and focused. You often need to be the center of attention.

EARTH
Pragmatic and down-to-earth, you are good at managing tasks and getting things done.

AIR
You live in your head, focusing on thoughts and ideas. Your task is to turn ideas into reality.

WATER
You think with your heart and may find it hard to be neutral. You understand how others feel.

THE POLARITIES IN YOUR CHART

High in positive/ low in negative

You like to be involved in the busy flow of life. Spending quiet time alone is a bigger challenge.

High in negative/ low in positive

You may be a little introverted; the inner world is more natural to you than the buzz of the outside world.

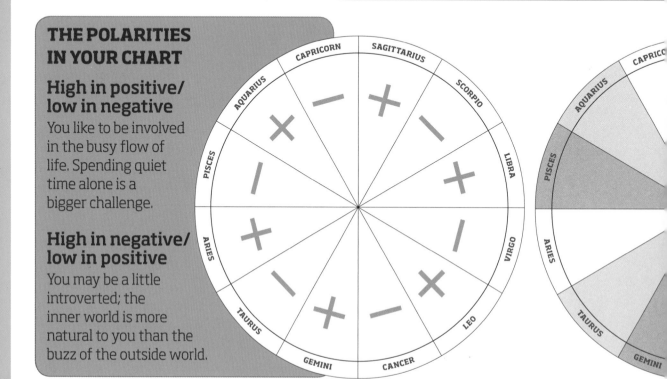

LOW

You find it hard to assert yourself or to be confident, yet you might find yourself having to lead.

It might be difficult for you to do what's best for your physical health. You may be subconsciously materialistic.

Too much talking is not your style. It may be hard for you to look at situations objectively.

Big displays of emotion don't come naturally to you. Inwardly, your emotions can be very forceful.

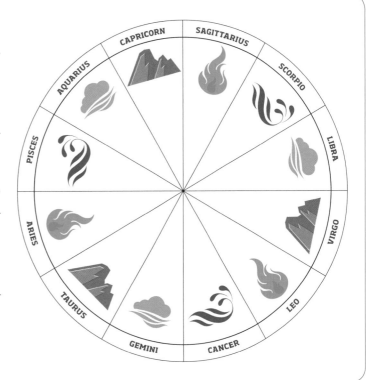

THE MODES IN YOUR CHART

MODE	HIGH	LOW
Cardinal ▷	You like to take the initiative and not be at the mercy of someone else's plans. It is important for you to set and meet goals.	Without realizing it, you may be drawn toward situations that require you to lead. You have to work to develop these skills.
Fixed ▷	Your skill is providing stability, but you can become afraid to move on. Coping with change will be a skill to learn.	It might be hard for you to stand your ground. Your challenge may be to stick with something.
Mutable ▷	You are very adaptable—sometimes too much so. You may give in too easily and like to go with the flow.	Your responses are clear and direct. It might be a challenge to feel content in situations where you are not in control.

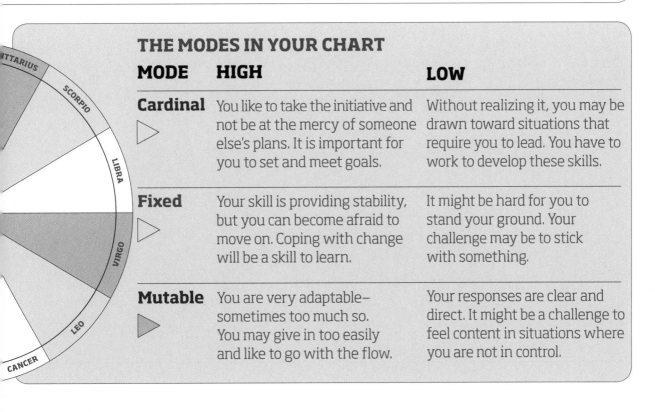

"**THE WHOLE POINT**
OF ASTROLOGY
IS TO LEARN
SOMETHING
ABOUT
WHAT YOU ARE."

Liz Greene,
Astrology for Lovers

THE **1ST** SIGN OF THE ZODIAC

ARIES

MARCH 21–APRIL 20

Aries is strong and full of vitality, like its animal, the ram. People who are Aries tend to be extroverted and like to take charge. They need action and know how to get a job done.

Symbol ♈
Polarity **Positive**
Mode **Cardinal**
Element **Fire**
Ruling planet **Mars**
Parts of the body **Head and adrenal glands**

Aries in the sky

The constellation of Aries is not always easy to pick out when viewing the sky. Its most recognizable feature is a crooked line of three stars: Alpha, Beta, and Gamma. In Greek mythology, Aries represents the ram whose golden fleece hung on a tree near the Black Sea. Jason and the Argonauts went on an epic voyage to bring this fleece back to Greece.

The three brightest star of Aries–Alpha, Beta, and Gamma–form a crooked line

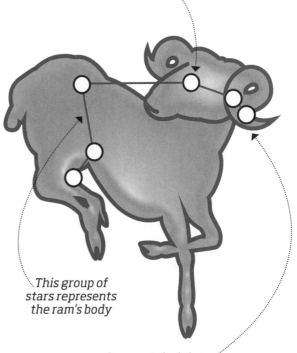

This group of stars represents the ram's body

Gamma Arietis is a double star with almost identical white components

THE **1ST** SIGN OF THE ZODIAC

ARIES

MARCH 21–APRIL 20

The Sun in Aries

If the Sun is in the Aries section of your chart, Aries is your "Sun sign." You like to be a pioneer and lead the way, breaking new ground for others to follow. As a courageous person, you search for ways to prove yourself.

Your planets in Aries

Planets in the Aries section of your chart will act with daring–you take charge in the aspects of your life these planets represent.

Aries on the cusp of a house

If Aries is right at the beginning point of a house, this is an area of life where you are competitive and self-motivated, willing to take risks and try new things.

TONS OF ENERGY Aries marks the start of spring in the Northern Hemisphere. The planets in this sign will show Aries' spirit and energy.

BRAVE & FEARLESS

This sign enjoys risk. Your planets here will seek out danger as a means of testing and proving their strength.

THE WARRIOR

THE RULER OF ARIES IS THE WARRIOR GOD MARS, WHICH IS WHY ARIENS ARE COMPETITIVE AND MOTIVATED TO WIN!

CHILDLIKE

This sign is straightforward and sometimes naïve. An Aries can be upset when others aren't honest and upfront, or when things do not go as planned.

SHOWING INITIATIVE

If you have the Sun or Moon in Aries, you probably like to take action and be the leader of the pack.

NEGATIVE TRAITS

The ram can be prone to "locking horns" or acting like a "battering ram"–Aries knows how to accomplish tasks, but can cause conflict.

HASTY

Planets here thrive on self-generated energy, but sometimes act without thinking things through.

IMPATIENT

YOU KNOW WHAT YOU WANT– AND YOU WANT IT RIGHT NOW!

GOING SOLO

WITH PLANETS IN ARIES, YOU LIKE TO WORK ALONE.

GOOD UNDER PRESSURE

Aries are clearheaded and able to think quickly in an emergency.

FIGHTING SPIRIT WHERE ARIES FALLS IN YOUR CHART, YOU SHOW COMPETITIVENESS AND HATE TO GIVE UP.

THE **2ND** SIGN OF THE ZODIAC

TAURUS

APRIL 21–MAY 21

Taurus is calm and cool–the bull is slow to anger and slow to move. Taureans are reserved, stable, and don't like change. They are in tune with their physical side and with nature.

Symbol ♉
Polarity **Negative**
Mode **Fixed**
Element **Earth**
Ruling planet **Venus**
Parts of the body
Neck and throat

Taurus in the sky

Known since ancient times, the constellation Taurus is represented by just the front half of the bull. It includes two open star clusters (groups)—the Hyades and Pleiades. A bright red star, Aldebaran, marks one eye. Taurus is most easily seen during November and December. It is almost impossible to see in May and June because it is too close to the Sun.

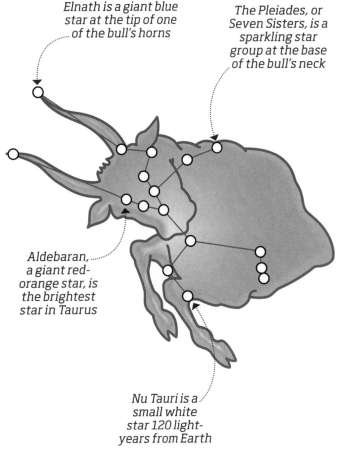

Elnath is a giant blue star at the tip of one of the bull's horns

The Pleiades, or Seven Sisters, is a sparkling star group at the base of the bull's neck

Aldebaran, a giant red-orange star, is the brightest star in Taurus

Nu Tauri is a small white star 120 light-years from Earth

THE **2ND** SIGN OF THE ZODIAC

TAURUS

APRIL 21–MAY 21

The Sun in Taurus

If the Sun is in the Taurus section of your chart, Taurus is your "Sun sign." Your goal is to create something you value, which will allow you to develop resilience. Like a garden, your work needs to be tended with care.

Your planets in Taurus

The planets in the Taurus section of your chart are grounded, but they also express the need for creative or artistic pursuits. This part of you requires time to consider and learn from experience. Beauty and art speak to you.

Taurus on the cusp of a house

If Taurus is right at the beginning point of a house, in this area of life, you are practical, committed, and persistent. You show you have the qualities of patience and endurance.

STEADY DOES IT After the spring rush of Aries, Taurus is calm and considered, slow and deliberate.

THE PHYSICAL WORLD

Taurians like simple sensory pleasures such as delicious food, music, and the arts.

PATIENCE A VIRTUE

ONE OF YOUR MOST VALUABLE SKILLS IS KNOWING THAT GOOD THINGS COME TO THOSE WHO WAIT. YOU CAN SIT BACK PATIENTLY WITH CALM ACCEPTANCE.

SLOW TO ANGER

Taureans are known for being calm—most of the time! But you can have a temper when pushed.

ROMANTIC

Taurus is ruled by Venus, goddess of love. Your planets here respond to strong friendships and romance.

NEGATIVE TRAITS

The bull can be immensely stubborn, sometimes against its own best interests. As fixed earth, Taurus can at times be greedy or self-indulgent.

$ WISE

WITH PLANETS IN TAURUS, YOU WILL BE GOOD AT MANAGING MONEY.

POSSESSIVE

TAURIANS OFTEN HESITATE TO LET GO OF IDEAS, PEOPLE, AND OBJECTS.

LOVE OF SECURITY

A Taurean values stability and dislikes upheaval and change.

ENDURING & PERSISTENT ONCE YOU HAVE COMMITTED YOURSELF TO A COURSE OF ACTION, YOU CAN BE RELIED ON TO STICK WITH IT.

THE **3RD** SIGN OF THE ZODIAC

GEMINI

MAY 22–JUNE 21

Gemini is sociable and outgoing, light and playful. People with the "twin" sign, however, are also easily bored. They have curious minds and need lots of variety and stimulation.

Symbol ♊
Polarity **Positive**
Mode **Mutable**
Element **Air**
Ruling planet **Mercury**
Parts of the body
Arms, hands, and lungs

Gemini in the sky

Gemini's two brightest stars, Castor and Pollux, make identifying this constellation easy. They are named for the twins of Greek mythology that Gemini represents. Castor and Pollux mark the heads of the twins, but they are not identical. Pollux, the brighter of the pair, is an orange giant 34 light-years away. Castor is a blue-white star 52 light-years away.

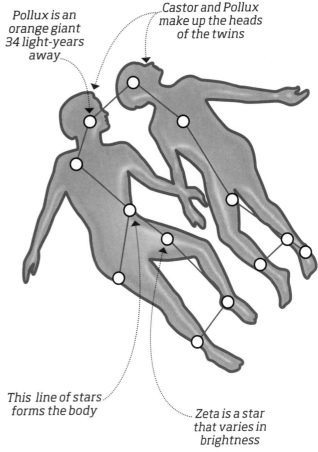

Pollux is an orange giant 34 light-years away

Castor and Pollux make up the heads of the twins

This line of stars forms the body

Zeta is a star that varies in brightness

THE **3RD** SIGN OF THE ZODIAC

GEMINI

MAY 22–JUNE 21

The Sun in Gemini

If the Sun is in the Gemini section of your chart, Gemini is your "Sun sign." You need to find your "twin." Every Gemini has light and dark sides, and it is your task to find out about both characters within yourself.

Your planets in Gemini

The planets in the Gemini section of your chart tend to adapt themselves easily to new environments and situations. Here, you will need to express yourself with lightness.

Gemini on the cusp of a house

If Gemini is right at the beginning point of a house, this is an area of life where you apply logic rather than emotion. You are curious and you need continual change and mental stimulus.

LOOK WHO'S TALKING
The image of the twins shows a need for conversation and social contact.

PLAYFUL & FUN
As a Gemini, you can be flirtatious and get attention by being funny and making others laugh.

ALWAYS CURIOUS
GEMINIS ARE CURIOUS AND LOVE TO LEARN. THEY LIKE TO MEET NEW PEOPLE AND FIND OUT ABOUT DIFFERENT PLACES.

SOCIAL BUTTERFLY
With planets in Gemini, you make friends easily. Your social circle is likely to be wide and diverse.

TWO IN ONE
Sometimes thought to be two-faced, Geminis can find themselves as the go-between when friends take different sides.

NEGATIVE TRAITS
At worst, Gemini skims the surface, reluctant to explore deeper feelings and consequences. This sign can play one side against the other.

NETWORKING
For a Gemini, it's important to make connections to others, without getting tied to one group.

WHAT NEXT?
STAYING FOCUSED ON ONE HOBBY OR SCHOOL SUBJECT CAN BE TOUGH.

CHANGE IS GOOD
THE WORST THING FOR A GEMINI IS TO FEEL BORED BY ROUTINE.

SEEKING OUT STIMULATION
A restless need for movement, activity, and stimulation is common among Geminis.

LIGHT VS. DARK THE BRIGHT CELESTIAL TWIN AND THE DARK EARTHLY TWIN EXIST TOGETHER IN GEMINI. IT IS IMPORTANT TO RECOGNIZE BOTH.

THE **4TH** SIGN OF THE ZODIAC

CANCER

JUNE 22–JULY 22

Cancer is sensitive, clever, and not likely to give up easily. As its animal symbol suggests, a hard outer shell protects a vulnerable interior. People with this sign often act on their emotions.

Symbol ♋
Polarity **Negative**
Mode **Cardinal**
Element **Water**
Ruling planet **Moon**
Parts of the body
Breasts and stomach

Cancer in the sky

Cancer is the faintest of the 12 zodiac constellations. Its major star group, Praesepe, is also called the Beehive or Manger. It was named the Manger because the stars Gamma and Delta Cancri look like two donkeys feeding at a manger. In Greek mythology, Cancer the crab attacked Hercules during his fight with the Hydra. The crab was crushed during the struggle.

The Beehive was known to the ancient Greeks, who could see it as a misty spot in the sky

Two stars positioned opposite each other form the claws

A large open-star group is at the heart of Cancer

THE **4TH** SIGN OF THE ZODIAC

CANCER

JUNE 22–JULY 22

The Sun in Cancer

If the Sun is in the Cancer section of your chart, Cancer is your "Sun sign." You are likely a natural caregiver. You like to find your tribe and develop a central role within it. Close bonds with family and friends are important.

Your planets in Cancer

The planets in the Cancer section of your chart will show a self-protective quality, acting according to moods and feelings. These planets rely on intuition. Emotion is a ruling force.

Cancer on the cusp of a house

If Cancer is right at the beginning point of a house, this area of your life may form a place of safety away from the world. You look to protect and defend this special place.

CLOSE TIES Cancerians put a lot of emotion into people, places, and possessions. Separating from them can be difficult.

CARING

Cancerians are known to be sensitive and capable of understanding how others feel. As adults, many go on to work in healing and caring professions.

FAMILIAR FACES

PEOPLE WITH THIS SIGN LIKE TO FEEL THAT THEY'RE IN KNOWN TERRITORY—WITH FAMILY, FRIENDS, HOME, AND SCHOOL.

SEA CREATURES

Like the tides, Cancer is ruled by the Moon, which means that energy and emotions go up and down.

EASILY HURT

Cancerians are sensitive and can lash out when their feelings are hurt or they become stressed and anxious.

FEELINGS

THE CANCERIAN STYLE IS ALL ABOUT PERSONAL EMOTIONS.

NEGATIVE TRAITS

Emotions often win out over common sense. Cancerians can be quick to take sides, and they don't always react well in unfamiliar situations.

POWERFUL INTUITION

People born under this sign easily pick up on emotional atmosphere and feelings.

NEED FOR SECURITY

PLANETS IN THIS SIGN NEED TO FEEL SAFE AND DON'T LIKE RISK.

KEEP AT IT!

When really set on an important goal, a Cancerian won't give up. They are determined, but not pushy.

WITHDRAWAL UNDER PRESSURE
CANCERIANS ACT ON INSTINCT, WITHDRAWING INTO THEIR SHELLS IF THEY SENSE DANGER.

THE **5TH** SIGN OF THE ZODIAC

LEO

JULY 23–AUGUST 22

Warm, bright, and charming, Leo has a regal air but is full of fun, too. People with a Leo Sun sign are confident, generous, motivated, and have a great sense of style.

Symbol ♌
Polarity **Positive**
Mode **Fixed**
Element **Fire**
Ruling planet **Sun**
Parts of the body
Heart and spine

Leo in the sky

The stars of Leo form the shape of a lion, representing the lion slain by Heracles of Greek mythology. A central group of stars represents the body, with branches for the lion's legs. Six stars form the lion's head and chest in a shape that looks like a backward question mark. This asterism (a pattern formed by stars in a constellation) is called the Sickle.

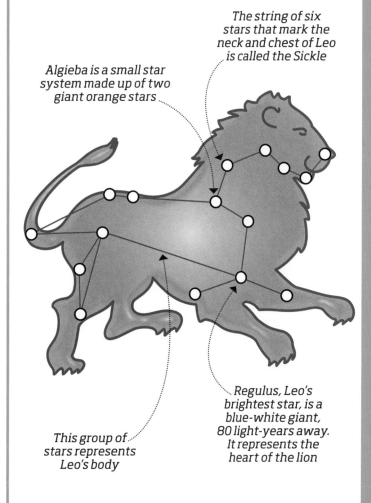

The string of six stars that mark the neck and chest of Leo is called the Sickle

Algieba is a small star system made up of two giant orange stars

This group of stars represents Leo's body

Regulus, Leo's brightest star, is a blue-white giant, 80 light-years away. It represents the heart of the lion

THE **5TH** SIGN OF THE ZODIAC

LEO

JULY 23–AUGUST 22

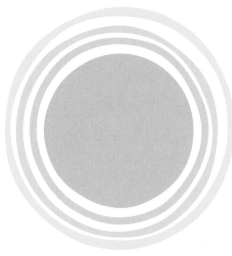

The Sun in Leo

If the Sun is in the Leo section of your chart, Leo is your "Sun sign." You like to develop your creativity and take center stage or lead the pack. You'll attract loyalty in return for your inspiration, support, and strength.

Your planets in Leo

The planets in the Leo section of your chart will act with courage, pride, and a sense of performance. These planets shine with star quality, attracting praise from others.

Leo at the cusp of a house

If Leo is right at the beginning point of a house, this area of your life will be close to your heart, a place where you can shine and develop your creativity. You put lots of energy into this, seeking praise and approval.

SENSE OF FUN Leo is a playful sign; planets here are easygoing and fun. Grown-up Leos connect easily to the world of children.

BOLD & COURAGEOUS

Leos tend to be daring, independent, and confident. Planets here will be brave and full of spirit.

THE PERFORMER

LEO LOVES THE LIMELIGHT AND PUTS ON A SHOW—HERE, LEO THRIVES ON ATTENTION, ADMIRATION, AND RESPECT.

GLAMOUR & SPARKLE

Leos hate to get their hands dirty and prefer to give tasks to other people.

WARM & GENEROUS

Those with planets in Leo are generous with their time and energy and find it easy to motivate others.

NEGATIVE TRAITS

Leo may show arrogance and self-centeredness, or easily suffer hurt pride. It's important to remember that other people need attention, too.

CREATIVITY

Those with planets in Leo may need lots of creative projects and hobbies to make them stand out.

HONOR

IN A POSITION OF TRUST, LEOS ARE HONORABLE AND HONEST.

LOOKING TO THE FUTURE

Leos are positive and forward-looking—optimistic, confident, and full of hope.

NEED TO BE SEEN

LEOS TEND TO BE LARGER THAN LIFE AND NEED TO FEEL SPECIAL.

ME, MYSELF, AND I WITH THE SUN RULING THIS SIGN, LEOS ARE INDEPENDENT AND FOCUS ON ACHIEVING GOALS. THEY CAN HAVE A VERY STRONG SENSE OF SELF.

THE **6TH** SIGN OF THE ZODIAC

VIRGO
AUGUST 23–SEPTEMBER 22

Virgos like to bring order to situations, and they tackle tasks efficiently and with little fuss. They are practical and provide a helping hand where needed. People with this sign take pride in having useful skills.

Symbol ♍
Polarity **Negative**
Mode **Mutable**
Element **Earth**
Ruling planet **Mercury**
Part of the body
Digestive system

Virgo in the sky

The figure of Virgo is named for a maiden goddess. What this large constellation lacks in bright star groups, it makes up for in the number of the galaxies it contains. Virgo can be seen equally well in both the Northern and Southern hemispheres. It is especially bright in springtime. The Virgo group of galaxies lies 50 million light-years away.

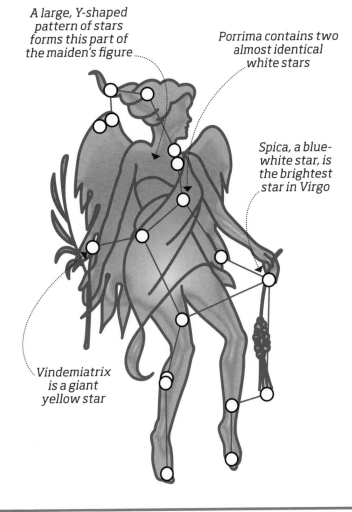

A large, Y-shaped pattern of stars forms this part of the maiden's figure

Porrima contains two almost identical white stars

Spica, a blue-white star, is the brightest star in Virgo

Vindemiatrix is a giant yellow star

THE **6TH** SIGN OF THE ZODIAC

VIRGO
AUGUST 23–SEPTEMBER 22

The Sun in Virgo

If the Sun is in the Virgo section of your chart, Virgo is your "Sun sign." Your goal is to perfect your chosen hobby or area of study. You feel happiest being a useful member of a team. Virgo Sun loves practical communication.

Your planets in Virgo

The planets in the Virgo section of you chart will not act in a showy way. This sign is not about drama. It focuses on being efficient and developing necessary skills.

Virgo on the cusp of a house

If Virgo is right at the beginning point of a house, this area of your life will run like a well-oiled machine–or you would like it to! Here, you seek to set order.

HELPING HAND This humble sign brings us down to earth after the glitz of Leo. While Leo loves a party, it's Virgo who will organize it.

SKILLFUL

The symbol of Virgo is the Virgin. In the ancient world, she watched over the harvest and used her skills to produce food. She is often shown holding a sheaf of wheat.

PERFECTIONISM

DOING A JOB WELL MATTERS TO VIRGOS. THEY EXPECT NOTHING LESS THAN PERFECTION FROM THEMSELVES.

EFFICIENT & PRACTICAL

Virgos are usually good at organizing tasks. They also focus on serving others in practical ways.

HUMBLE & CAPABLE

A sense of self-worth comes from being useful and productive. However, Virgos run the risk of underestimating their talents.

A SENSE OF ORDER

Virgo's role is to establish and work according to a system. Those who have planets in this sign will dislike chaos.

JUST SO

WHEN TAKING ON AN ASSIGNMENT, VIRGOS GET THE DETAILS RIGHT.

NEGATIVE TRAITS

Virgos can get lost in the details and don't always see the big picture. Sweating the small stuff can turn into an unhealthy need for control.

SORTING INFO

Virgos have a flair for managing information and putting it to good use. They are valued project leaders.

HEAD SPACE

WITHOUT TIME TO RELAX, VIRGOS CAN BECOME STRESSED.

HEALTH AND WELL-BEING FOR VIRGOS, MIND AND BODY ARE LINKED. EXERCISE AND HEALTHY EATING HELP KEEP THE MIND AND BODY IN TOP SHAPE.

"WE COME **SPINNING** OUT OF NOTHINGNESS, SCATTERING **STARS LIKE DUST**."

Jalal ad-Din Rumi

THE **7TH** SIGN OF THE ZODIAC

LIBRA

SEPTEMBER 23–OCTOBER 22

Outgoing and social, Librans are good at creating relationships. The scales indicate a need for harmony and balance. Those with this sign are diplomatic and fair and often have an artistic flair.

Symbol ♎

Polarity **Positive**

Mode **Cardinal**

Element **Air**

Ruling planet **Venus**

Part of the body **Kidneys**

Libra in the sky

A constellation of the zodiac between Virgo and Scorpius, Libra represents the scales of justice held by Virgo. It is the only zodiac constellation based on an object, not an animal or character from mythology. The ancient Greeks saw the constellation as the claws of the neighboring scorpion, Scorpius. For this reason, its two brightest stars are named the Northern and Southern Claw.

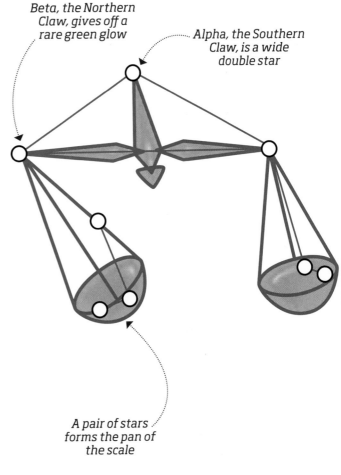

Beta, the Northern Claw, gives off a rare green glow

Alpha, the Southern Claw, is a wide double star

A pair of stars forms the pan of the scale

THE **7TH** SIGN OF THE ZODIAC

LIBRA

SEPTEMBER 23–OCTOBER 22

The Sun in Libra

If the Sun is in the Libra section of your chart, Libra is your "Sun sign." You have a highly developed sense of fairness and are often a go-between with others. You have a sense of poise and grace.

Your planets in Libra

The planets in the Libra section of your chart will express themselves with good manners, seeking to create harmony and acting in a considerate way toward others.

Libra on the cusp of a house

If Libra is right at the beginning point of a house, this is an area of life where you work to be diplomatic. Here, you are good at sharing or working in tandem with someone else.

THE SCALES The scales of justice reflect Libra's function of creating a peaceful atmosphere and perfect balance.

TACT & DIPLOMACY

Librans hate to upset anyone or rock the boat. They prefer to win people over with good manners and charm.

FAIR-MINDED

THIS SIGN IS CONCERNED WITH FAIRNESS AND EQUALITY. LIBRANS ARE OFTEN DRAWN TO SUPPORT SOCIAL CAUSES.

BEAUTY AND APPEARANCE

An appreciation of fine things and style are found here. Outer beauty reflects inner harmony.

INDECISIVE

The Libran spirit tries to see all points of view and be objective. The desire to be fair can make it hard to make decisions.

BY THE BOOK

Librans, sometimes called "polite Aries," follow the rules. They will challenge someone who breaks rules or who behaves unfairly.

NEGATIVE TRAITS

Perhaps your least attractive quality is insincerity–although you may really be trying to keep the peace and make situations and people look good.

UMPIRE

FAIR AND POLITE, LIBRANS ARE GOOD REFS IN DISPUTES AMONG FRIENDS.

THE ART OF COMPROMISE

Librans will often give ground if this results in peace and happiness all around.

PEOPLE PERSON

A LIBRAN'S SPIRIT SINKS DURING TIMES OF SOLITUDE.

THE ARTSY TYPE AS A VENUS-RULED SIGN, LIBRA HAS A STRONG TIE WITH THE ARTS—MANY LIBRANS ARE GIFTED ARTISTS, MUSICIANS, AND FASHIONISTAS.

THE **8TH** SIGN OF THE ZODIAC

SCORPIO
OCTOBER 23-NOVEMBER 21

Scorpios are complex people, passionate about their interests and relationships. Yet, they also have great self-control. The saying "still waters run deep" is a good way to describe those with this sign.

Symbol ♏
Polarity **Negative**
Mode **Fixed**
Element **Water**
Ruling planets **Mars and Pluto**
Parts of the body **Reproductive organs and eliminatory system**

Scorpio in the sky

Scorpius represents the scorpion that in Greek mythology was sent by the goddess Artemis to kill Orion. Scorpius is easy to recognize. The heart of the beast is marked by the supergiant red star Antares, which is hundreds of times larger than the Sun. A curve of stars represents the tail—ready to strike. Other stars form the head and claws.

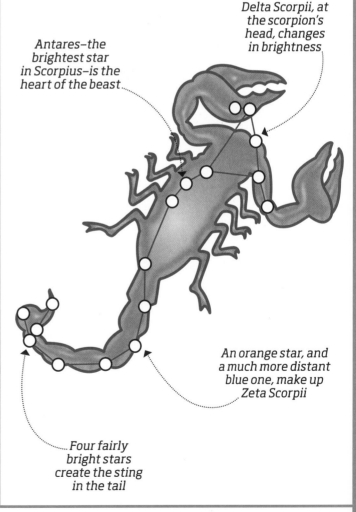

Delta Scorpii, at the scorpion's head, changes in brightness

Antares–the brightest star in Scorpius–is the heart of the beast

An orange star, and a much more distant blue one, make up Zeta Scorpii

Four fairly bright stars create the sting in the tail

THE **8TH** SIGN OF THE ZODIAC

SCORPIO
OCTOBER 23-NOVEMBER 21

The Sun in Scorpio

If the Sun is in the Scorpio section of your chart, Scorpio is your "Sun sign." You know the importance of being resilient. You will work to overcome obstacles and your "solar gold" is the inner strength this brings.

Your planets in Scorpio

The planets in the Scorpio section of your chart will act with passion, intensity, and quiet courage. After a setback, you are renewed in a purer and stronger form.

Scorpio on the cusp of a house

If Scorpio is right at the beginning point of a house, this is an area of life that is subject to cycles of crisis, removal, and renewal.

TAKING IT TO THE LIMIT This sign admires emotional courage and the ability to survive by one's own intelligence.

WILLPOWER & STRENGTH

The symbol for Scorpio is the scorpion, a creature able to withdraw into itself to survive the most extreme conditions.

INNER CONTROL

A SCORPIO WON'T ADMIT TO FEELING POWERLESS. SELF-CONTROL IS VALUED ABOVE NEARLY ALL ELSE.

SECRETIVE & PRIVATE

Scorpio is often the strong, silent type, unwilling to say how they truly feel. Showing emotion is hard.

POSSESSIVE

Scorpios may be possessive. On the plus side, people with this sign show true loyalty. They can, unfortunately, also show jealousy.

DEEP THINKER

Scorpios often enjoy doing research into complex subjects. Studies in areas like archaeology and psychology fascinate!

NEGATIVE TRAITS

Once hurt, it is hard for those with this sign to forgive or forget. Betrayal cuts deep and sometimes the instinct is for revenge. This sign may try to control others.

DETECTIVE

WITH A STRONG SIXTH SENSE, THE SCORPIO MAKES A GOOD SLEUTH.

EMOTIONAL HONESTY

SCORPIOS ARE INTUITIVE. THEY SEE INTO THE HEART OF THINGS.

A STING IN THE TAIL

It is hard to admit defeat. This trait makes Scorpio a worthy opponent.

COOL CHARACTER SCORPIOS POSSESS POWERFUL EMOTIONS, WHICH ARE USUALLY HIDDEN BENEATH WHAT SEEMS LIKE A DETACHED EXTERIOR.

THE **9TH** SIGN OF THE ZODIAC

SAGITTARIUS
NOVEMBER 22–DECEMBER 21

The Sagittarian spirit is optimistic and forward-looking. These wanderers feel at home wherever they go. People with this sign are sociable and restless, needing lots of space to spread their wings.

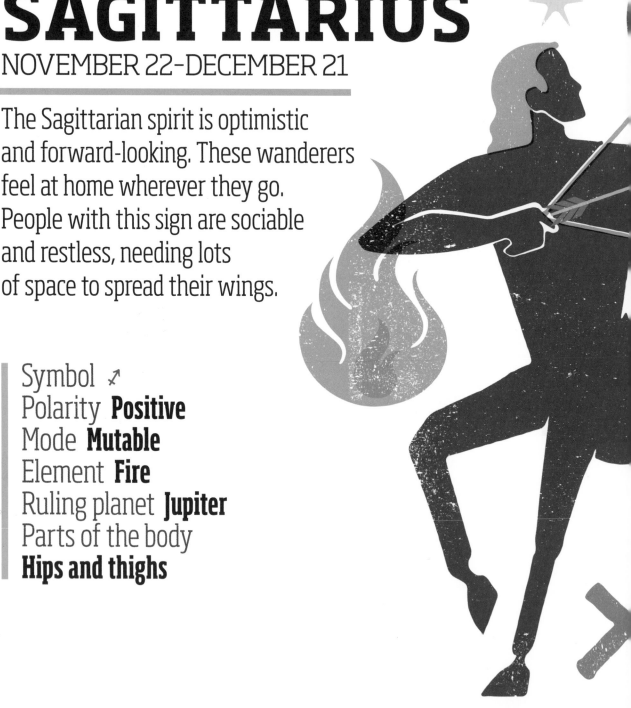

Symbol ♐

Polarity **Positive**

Mode **Mutable**

Element **Fire**

Ruling planet **Jupiter**

Parts of the body
Hips and thighs

Sagittarius in the sky

Sagittarius is a major constellation. It lies near the center of the Milky Way and is home to many star groups. The constellation figure of Sagittarius shows a centaur (half-man, half-horse) holding an archer's bow. To find Sagittarius in the sky, it may help to identify the Teapot asterism—a pattern of stars at the center of the constellation that looks like a teapot.

The top of the bow area has impressive bright nebulae

Pi Sagittarii marks the back of the archer's head

This central area is the Teapot asterism

Kaus Australis, the brightest star, is 153 light-years away

THE **9TH** SIGN OF THE ZODIAC

SAGITTARIUS
NOVEMBER 22–DECEMBER 21

The Sun in Sagittarius

If the Sun is in the Sagittarius section of your chart, Sagittarius is your "Sun sign." Your passion is to explore, discover, and have adventures. This is a philosophical sign; with the Sun here, you are looking for deep meaning.

Your planets in Sagittarius

The planets in the Sagittarius section of your chart radiate fiery confidence. You look to the future and need a lot of freedom to find your way. You do not react well to restrictions.

Sagittarius on the cusp of a house

If Sagittarius is right at the beginning point of a house, this is an area of your life that can't wait to go exploring. You are excited to find out what awaits in the wider world.

ARCHER The symbol of the archer shows an arrow shot into the distance. Sagittarians are excited by potential and possibility.

LOOKING AHEAD

Sagittarians boldly look to the future and are good at finding new opportunities.

SPLIT NATURE

SAGITTARIUS IS RULED BY UPBEAT JUPITER. THOSE BORN UNDER THE SIGN HAVE A SUNNY OPTIMISM, BUT A DARK SIDE, TOO.

WHAT DOES IT ALL MEAN?

At the heart of this sign's wanderings is a search for meaning—a need to answer life's big questions.

THE GREAT OUTDOORS

Those born with this sign strong in their chart love sports and nature.

NEGATIVE TRAITS

Sagittarius is not noted for its carefulness or precision. This can result in an unorganized approach to problem-solving.

OPEN MIND

Long-distance travel, education, religion, and philosophy can all be appealing to Sagittarians.

HONEST

SAGITTARIAN HONESTY CAN SEEM BLUNT TO OTHERS.

DON'T FENCE ME IN

THE NEED FOR FREEDOM CAN SHOW AS A LACK OF FOLLOW-THROUGH AND COMMITMENT.

THE CENTAUR

Sagittarius is linked to the Centaur, a mythical half-horse and half-man. This suggests a love of both wild nature and deep thought.

OPTIMISTIC OUTLOOK A FIRE SIGN, SAGITTARIUS POSSESSES THE CONFIDENCE TO BELIEVE THAT EVERYTHING WILL WORK OUT FINE IN THE END.

THE **10TH** SIGN OF THE ZODIAC

CAPRICORN
DECEMBER 22–JANUARY 19

Capricorn is focused and hardworking, aiming for practical achievements and success. People with this sign work patiently and steadily toward a clear target before moving swiftly on to the next task. They can be introverts.

Symbol ♑
Polarity **Negative**
Mode **Cardinal**
Element **Earth**
Ruling planet **Saturn**
Parts of the body **Knees, teeth, bones, and skin**

Capricorn in the sky

Capricornus lies in the southern sky between Sagittarius and Aquarius. In Greek myth, Capricornus represents the goatlike god Pan. In one tale of his adventures, he jumped into a river and turned himself into a creature that was part fish to escape from the sea monster Typhon. This is why the constellation is shown as a goat with the tail of a fish.

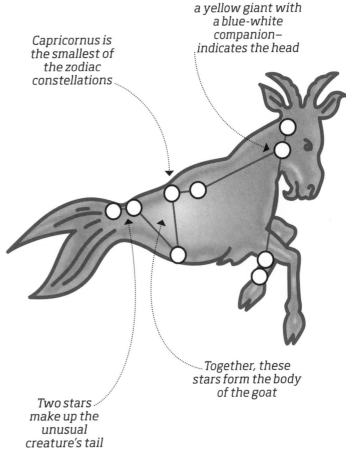

A wide double star– a yellow giant with a blue-white companion– indicates the head

Capricornus is the smallest of the zodiac constellations

Together, these stars form the body of the goat

Two stars make up the unusual creature's tail

THE **10TH** SIGN OF THE ZODIAC

CAPRICORN

DECEMBER 22–JANUARY 19

The Sun in Capricorn

If the Sun is in the Capricorn section of your chart, Capricorn is your "Sun sign." You work on self-reliance, taking on responsibility for yourself and others. The path may be lonely at times, but you keep your eye on the prize.

Your planets in Capricorn

The planets in the Capricorn section of your chart will act with mature dignity, aware of tradition and what is socially acceptable. You develop these gifts slowly over time.

Capricorn on the cusp of a house

If Capricorn is right at the beginning point of a house, you show maturity and seek respect from others. You act practically, with an eye to material gain. You work with purpose and structure in this area.

PLAYING BY THE RULES This is a conservative sign. Capricorn understands the rules, and, in fact, probably wrote them!

DETERMINED

CAPRICORN'S ANIMAL IS THE GOAT. IT SHOWS THIS SIGN'S AMBITIOUS CLIMB TO THE TOP AND ITS QUIET ENDURANCE.

HARD WORKER

This sign expects things to be tough and happily knuckles down. Capricorns want to feel they've earned what they get.

NEGATIVE TRAITS

This sign can be overly serious and rigid at times. This can mean being strategic–but sometimes ruthless and calculating, too.

SELF-SUFFICIENT

Capricorns prefer not to rely on others. They can be independent and good at setting goals.

WORLDLY & PRACTICAL

Saving for the future and being good with money are important. The focus is on things more than ideas.

GOAT-FISH

This is an ancient symbol of the Mesopotamian god of civilization and earthly abundance.

PLANNERS

CAPRICORNS LIKE TO PLAN AHEAD AND KNOW WHAT TO EXPECT.

TAKING ON RESPONSIBILITY

Capricorn is organized and reliable. Status and position are important, too.

USEFUL TALENTS

CAPRICORNS FOCUS ON PRACTICAL SKILLS WITH REAL-WORLD USES.

SENSE OF PURPOSE CAPRICORNS ARE HAPPIEST WITH CLEAR GOALS, STRUCTURE, AND A SENSE OF CONCRETE ACHIEVEMENT. PURPOSEFUL WORK IS KEY.

THE **11TH** SIGN OF THE ZODIAC

AQUARIUS

JANUARY 20–FEBRUARY 18

Highly independent, Aquarius is also a social sign. People with this sign are outgoing and like to be part of a group. Aquarians often have a strong sense of social justice and care about the well-being of others.

Symbol ♒
Polarity **Positive**
Mode **Fixed**
Element **Air**
Ruling planets **Saturn and Uranus**
Parts of the body **Shins and ankles**

Aquarius in the sky

Aquarius is called the Water Bearer. The figure represents a young man pouring water from a jar. The constellation contains two planetary nebulae (glowing gas thrown off by red giant stars as they die). The Saturn Nebula is just below a star near the left hand. The Helix Nebula lies south of the figure. Another star group (M2) is found by the head.

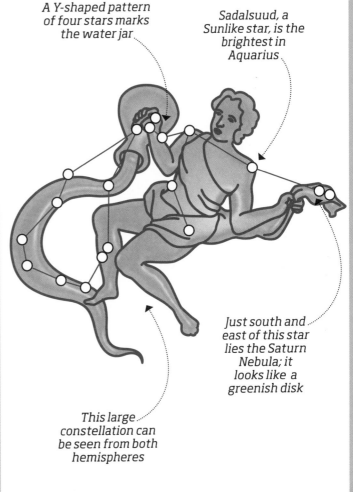

A Y-shaped pattern of four stars marks the water jar

Sadalsuud, a Sunlike star, is the brightest in Aquarius

Just south and east of this star lies the Saturn Nebula; it looks like a greenish disk

This large constellation can be seen from both hemispheres

THE **11TH** SIGN OF THE ZODIAC

AQUARIUS

JANUARY 20–FEBRUARY 18

The Sun in Aquarius

If the Sun is in the Aquarius section of your chart, Aquarius is your "Sun sign." Your goal is to find your place within a group, while holding on to your own views. You care deeply about fairness and equality.

Your planets in Aquarius

People with planets in the Aquarius section of their chart usually march to the beat of their own drum. Planets here tend to be cool and reserved.

Aquarius on the cusp of a house

If Aquarius is right at the beginning point of a house, you are likely to approach this area of your life in a highly individual way, forming your own ideas and ignoring the conventional way of doing things.

IDEALISTIC AQUARIUS
Aquarians are often leaders of change, with idealistic views of how things should be.

COMMUNITY SPIRIT
Aquarians tend to thrive in groups and communities that are working together toward a shared goal.

UNCONVENTIONAL
PLANETS IN AQUARIUS DON'T FOLLOW TRENDS. THEY PREFER TO EXPRESS THEMSELVES IN THEIR OWN UNIQUE WAY.

RATIONAL & CLEAR
Aquarians can be awkward with emotion. Logical conversation is preferred.

GROUP DYNAMIC
It can be difficult for those in this sign to honor personal creative power and still do what's best for the group.

NEGATIVE TRAITS
A feeling of intellectual superiority can sometimes get in the way of a truly democratic outlook.

RATIONAL INTELLIGENCE
A gift for rational thinking often feeds an interest in science or technology.

SPEAK OUT
FREEDOM OF EXPRESSION IS ESSENTIAL TO CREATIVITY.

FRIENDSHIPS
RELATIONSHIPS MUST HONOR THE NEED FOR SPACE AND FREEDOM.

RULE BREAKER?
Co-rulership of Saturn and Uranus means this sign acknowledges rules but doesn't always play by them.

FAIRNESS AQUARIUS REPRESENTS THE IDEAL OF A FAIR SOCIETY. ITS SYMBOL, THE WATER BEARER, POURS OUT THE WATERS OF KNOWLEDGE FOR THE BENEFIT OF ALL.

THE **12TH** SIGN OF THE ZODIAC

PISCES
FEBRUARY 19–MARCH 20

People born under this sign are focused on an internal world of imagination and feelings. They find a strong connection to stories and the magical world. This sign values ideas and people over material goods.

Symbol ♓
Polarity **Negative**
Mode **Mutable**
Element **Water**
Ruling planet **Jupiter and Neptune**
Parts of the body **Feet**

Pisces in the sky

In Greek myth, Pisces represents the goddess Aphrodite and her son, Eros. In the story, they transformed into fish and jumped into the Euphrates River to escape a monster named Typhon. In the constellation, the two fish are tied together but moving in different directions. One is moving toward the human and earthly; the other is trying to escape and head toward the spititual.

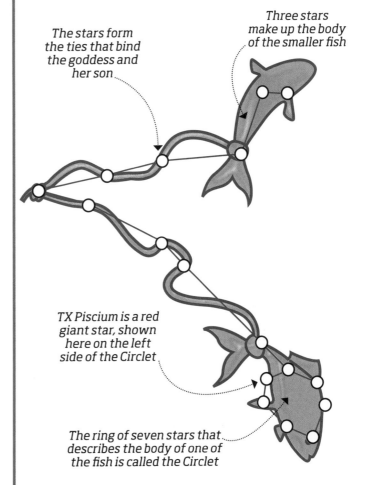

The stars form the ties that bind the goddess and her son

Three stars make up the body of the smaller fish

TX Piscium is a red giant star, shown here on the left side of the Circlet

The ring of seven stars that describes the body of one of the fish is called the Circlet

THE **12TH** SIGN OF THE ZODIAC

PISCES

FEBRUARY 19–MARCH 20

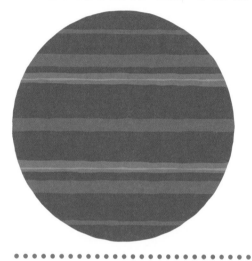

The Sun in Pisces

If the Sun is in the Pisces section of your chart, Pisces is your "Sun sign." You want to give service to a higher principle, which may mean putting aside personal desires. Developing artistry and imagination are important.

Your planets in Pisces

People with planets in the Pisces section of their chart can be unfocused. They are moved by subtle feelings rather than practical matters and may lack boundaries.

Pisces on the cusp of a house

If Pisces is right at the beginning point of a house, imagination is a big part of this area of your life. Here, you might be inspired to acts of devotion or want to follow your intuition.

MAGIC & ENCHANTMENT

Pisceans are known for their vivid imaginations. This sign is drawn to the make believe of enchanted worlds.

SENSITIVE & RECEPTIVE

A Piscean keenly senses moods around them, often feeling overwhelmed by outside emotions.

HARD TO PIN DOWN

IT MAY BE A CHALLENGE TO COMMIT TO LONG-TERM GOALS OR OBLIGATIONS THAT GIVE THE FEELING OF BEING TIED DOWN.

ARTISTIC & IMAGINATIVE

People in this sign may feel like fish out of water if they can't use creativity.

DOWNTIME

Sensitivity and a dislike of pressure mean a need for quiet. It's important to recharge physical and emotional batteries.

GIVING NATURE

Pisceans may be involved in charity work and in helping others. They are likely drawn to situations where they can assist.

WORLD OF DREAMS

Dreams, myths, fantasies, and stories may feel more real than ordinary life.

CARER

COMPASSIONATE AND DEVOTED, PISCES WANTS TO SAVE THE WORLD.

FAST FRIENDS

IN FRIENDSHIPS, PISCEANS ARE IDEALISTIC AND ATTENTIVE.

NEGATIVE TRAITS

A Piscean sometimes drifts or lets themselves be taken advantage of. Losing faith and wanting to be rescued can be weaknesses.

NEED TO ESCAPE PISCES' SYMBOL IS THE TWO FISH TIED TOGETHER. ONE SWIMS WITH ITS GAZE TURNED UPWARD, LONGING TO ESCAPE THE ORDINARY WORLD.

THE
PLANETS

The Sun

Mercury
Venus
The Moon orbiting Earth
Mars

Jupiter

Saturn

Chiron

THE ROLE OF THE PLANETS

The planets are like actors in your chart. Each plays a part, representing a universal human trait that exists in you. The relationships between the planets in your chart form the heart of your personality.

SHINE | NURTURE | COMMUNICATE | RELATE | ASSE

PERSONAL PLANETS

SOCIAL PLANETS

The Sun	**The Moon**	**Mercury**	**Venus**	**Mars**	**Jupiter**
The central core of our being	Our instinctual responses and caring principle	How we think, learn, and communicate	The principle of pleasure and of relating	How we defend ourselves and direct our energy	The principle of faith and optimism

A picture of you

In a birth chart, a planet represents a basic need and how you express it. Venus, for instance, represents beauty and harmony.

Each person's chart contains every planet, but the planets occupy different zodiac signs and houses. They all have a relationship to each other around the wheel of the chart (the "aspects"). Each chart gives a picture of a person.

Three planet groups

Astrology divides the planets into three groups, based on their distance from the Sun.

The "personal planets" include the Sun, the Moon, Mercury, Venus, and Mars. (In astrology,

the Sun and Moon are treated as planets.) Daytime is ruled by the Sun, and the Moon governs the night. They represent our character and play the central role in our chart.

Jupiter and Saturn are "social planets." They represent socialization in the family and in society. Jupiter oversees education, travel, and religion. Saturn has us adjust to society's rules.

Uranus, Neptune, and Pluto are "transpersonal" planets, spending a long time in each sign. The sign they occupy describes political and social ideals of an era. Chiron unites personal, social, and collective themes.

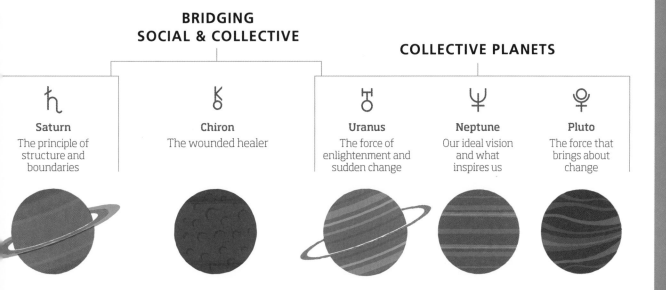

BRIDGING SOCIAL & COLLECTIVE

COLLECTIVE PLANETS

Saturn
The principle of structure and boundaries

Chiron
The wounded healer

Uranus
The force of enlightenment and sudden change

Neptune
Our ideal vision and what inspires us

Pluto
The force that brings about change

THE SUN

IDENTITY AND LIFE PURPOSE

The Sun is at the center of the solar system, and the astrological Sun is at the heart of the birth chart. It is the Sun that drives our personal development and creativity, with the other planets acting in support.

The Sun in the sky

The Sun provides us with light and warmth. It measures the days with its rising and setting. We count years with the cycle of the seasons. The Sun is our source of life and energy, and everything revolves around it.

The Sun in myth

Solar gods and goddesses brought light and vitality to the world. The ancient Greek god Helios drove the Sun chariot across the sky. Other Sun gods that represent the life-giving force of the Sun are the Egyptian Ra, Celtic Lugh, and Hindu Surya.

The Sun in the world around us

Bright yellow and orange flowers turn toward the Sun and follow it in the sky. St. John's wort, a plant used to improve people's mood, falls under the Sun. This planet symbolizes monarchs, presidents, leaders, and fathers.

Rules **Leo**
Day of the week **Sunday**
Metal **Gold**
Colors **Gold, orange, yellow**
Symbol ☉

PURPOSE | CREATIVE POWER | PRIDE

HEART OF OUR BEING | GOALS

SHINING LIGHT | VITALITY | CONFIDENCE

THE SUN

IDENTITY AND LIFE PURPOSE

THE SUN **IN YOUR CHART**
The influence of this planet will be felt according to where it resides and its relationship to other planets.

PURPOSE The Sun is the source of all energy. We can develop our unique creativity by focusing that energy–on our studies, interests, and relationships.

PATH The Sun directs us toward our true path; the other planets lead us along it. We understand our nature once we have gained self-knowledge and seen our way forward.

PRIDE We want to be recognized and to develop meaningful talents. When we make the most of our talents, we contribute to our community through our achievements.

POTENTIAL Where the Sun is in our chart, we can be inspiring, or we can lack confidence or be arrogant. Our experiences can affect if we meet our potential or not.

THE SUN **THROUGH THE SIGNS**

Consider how this planet expresses itself according to the sign that it occupies.

Aries You may be called on to be brave and take charge. Tests of courage bring out your warrior spirit.

Taurus Your creative gift lies in your love of the physical world and nature. You want to build something that lasts.

Gemini Your identity is wrapped up in your language and communication skills. Knowledge is your goal.

Cancer Your gift is a highly developed sense of sensitivity and supportiveness. Caring comes naturally to you.

Leo You look to shine your light brightly and are an able leader. It is important for you to be admired.

Virgo You might be drawn to learning new talents and crafts. Your focus will be on skill and practicality.

Libra Finding harmony and balance is key for you. You may fulfill this need through art or relationships.

Scorpio You rely on inner strength to get you through tough times. Your experiences help you grow and change.

Sagittarius You are naturally curious about the world. You may love travel and learning about other cultures.

Capricorn You may have to take on a leadership role. It will help develop self-reliance and reliability.

Aquarius You have principles and are concerned with fairness and equality. You may thrive in a diverse community.

Pisces Using your imagination and developing your creative side gives you a sense of pride.

THE MOON

INSTINCT AND PROTECTION

The symbol for the Moon is the crescent Moon. It reminds us that the Moon reflects light from the Sun and doesn't shine its own light. In the chart, the Moon plays a smaller role than the Sun sign.

The Moon in the sky

Watching the Moon's cycle is magical. A few days after the new Moon, the Moon looks like a slim crescent in the sky. After, it waxes (increases) until at full Moon we see the complete shining disk. It then wanes (decreases) into darkness.

The Moon in myth

The Moon's cycle is compared to the life stages of a woman: maiden, mother, and old woman. The three Fates of Greek and Norse myth also represent the Moon's cycle. In astrology, the Moon is linked to birth, mothering, feeding, and caring.

The Moon in the world around us

The gravitational pull of the Moon governs the ocean tides. For this reason, it is connected to the oceans and water. Its phases are in line with natural rhythms. The Moon is tied to the body's autonomic processes, such as breathing.

Rules **Cancer**
Day of the week **Monday**
Metal **Silver**
Color **White, silver**
Symbol ☽

PHYSICAL | EMOTIONAL | INSTINCT | FEELINGS

RHYTHMS & RITUALS | MATERNAL

NURTURE | NATURE | SECURITY

THE MOON

INSTINCT AND PROTECTION

THE MOON **IN YOUR CHART**
The influence of this planet will be felt according to where it resides and its relationship to other planets.

INTUITION The Sun symbolizes bold self-discovery. The Moon tells us what we are by nature and how we act intuitively. The lunar and solar drives are best in balance.

NURTURING The Moon represents the mother figure in our lives. It shows how we create a relationship with someone who nurtures us, and how we care for others.

SELF-CARE Food falls under the Moon. How do we feed and care for ourselves? What makes us feel "fed" and satisfied? Eating habits may show deeper feelings.

RELATIONSHIPS You may have an immediate bond with friends. The Moon connects you to your "tribe," drawing you to people and places that feel like home.

THE MOON **THROUGH THE SIGNS**

Consider how this planet expresses itself according to the sign that it occupies.

Aries You do not like delay or waiting for others. You are independent and can lead the way.

Taurus It's best to take things slowly and calmly. You need contact with the natural world.

Gemini What feeds you is discussion. You like learning new information, reading, and talking about ideas.

Cancer You are concerned with security and protecting yourself and others. Strong feelings go up and down.

Leo You seek praise and love from others. You are likely to be very in touch with your creative talents.

Virgo You are practical and humble in your approach to helping others. Taking good care of yourself is vital, too.

Libra You like close relationships and don't really like going solo. Calm and peace are needed for happiness.

Scorpio Your emotions run deep, and you sometimes hold onto hurt feelings. Physical exercise helps clear your mind.

Sagittarius You need room to move around, both physically and emotionally. You value your freedom.

Capricorn You like routine and tend to be efficient with your time and energy. You like feeling in control.

Aquarius You are naturally outgoing and sociable. Being part of a group or community may be important to you.

Pisces It can be hard to express how you feel. You are sensitive to others' feelings. Time alone helps you recharge.

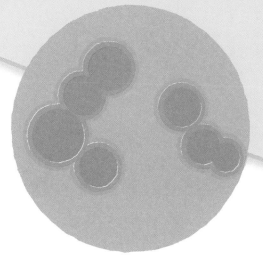

"A PERSON'S CHART IS THE DOOR OPENING US INTO THEIR MYTHICAL SYSTEM."

Richard Idemon,
Through the Looking Glass: A Search for the Self in the Mirror of Relationships

MERCURY

COMMUNICATION AND LEARNING

Mercury is our own personal "messenger." It describes how we see the world, the ways in which we learn, and how we communicate with others. Mercury strongly influences our perceptions of the world around us.

Mercury in the sky

Because it is so near to the Sun, Mercury can only occupy the same zodiac sign as the Sun or its neighboring sign. Three times a year, Mercury seems to disappear into the Sun's rays. This is why it is known as a trickster and underworld guide.

Mercury in myth

In Roman mythology, swift-footed Mercury was a god of language, writing, and invention. His Greek counterpart was Hermes, messenger of Zeus. Clever and skilled with his hands, Hermes made the first musical instrument.

Mercury in the world around us

Mercury covers anything connected to communication, such as books and phones. Types of transportation fit here, too—bikes, buses, or anything that takes us on short trips. Schools, stores, and markets also fall under Mercury.

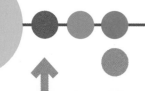

Rules **Gemini and Virgo**
Day of the week **Wednesday**
Metal **Mercury (quicksilver)**
Colors **Gray, multicolors**
Symbol ☿

COMMUNICATION | EDUCATION | SIBLINGS |

TRADE & BUSINESS | IDEAS

FACTUAL MEMORY | YOUTH | LANGUAGE

MERCURY

COMMUNICATION AND LEARNING

MERCURY **IN YOUR CHART**

The influence of this planet will be felt according to where it resides and its relationship to other planets.

COMMUNICATION Mercury helps us give voice to our thoughts and ideas. Through our words, we connect with other people and create bonds and friendships.

EDUCATION Education belongs to this planet. We all learn in different ways: your learning style may be structured or you may work best with a more free-flowing approach.

TRADE Mercury governs trade and business (the exchange of money and goods). For you, that could mean being treasurer of a club or budgeting your money.

YOUTHFUL This youthful planet is known for dexterity, craftsmanship, and ingenuity. Where Mercury is in our chart, we likely show curiousity and mischievousness.

MERCURY **THROUGH THE SIGNS**

Consider how this planet expresses itself according to the sign that it occupies.

Aries You are a clear thinker and decision-maker. Your communication style is direct and to the point.

Taurus Your thoughts tend to be unhurried and considered. You prefer learning and studying at your own pace.

Gemini You are always ready with a funny comment. Naturally curious, you may have varied interests and hobbies.

Cancer It's likely you have a great memory. You absorb information quickly and may be interested in history.

Leo You are extroverted and confident. You can keep an audience entertained with the power of your words.

Virgo You are orderly and organized in your thoughts. You might be gifted at working with your hands.

Libra You can charm and persuade others. At the same time, you give everyone's opinion equal time.

Scorpio You have a sharp mind and can sense what makes others tick. You are able to keep a secret. Privacy is key.

Sagittarius Your open-minded outlook and interest in others make you fun and interesting to be around.

Capricorn Your practical mind can complete tasks quickly. You favor structure and are goal-driven.

Aquarius You are likely to be interested in the sciences and have a logical mind. Truthfulness is important.

Pisces You have a vivid imagination and love making up stories. You learn best when able to be creative.

VENUS

LOVE AND PLEASURE

In our chart, Venus governs pleasure and affection. It reflects our notions of beauty and taste, in people and our surroundings. Venus indicates how we show love and how we create shared bonds.

- -

Venus in the sky

From our view on Earth, Venus is visible more often than Mercury. However, it does follow the same pattern of appearing east and then west of the Sun. In the east, it is the evening star; in the west, it is the morning star.

Venus in myth

This planet has been associated since ancient times with the goddess of love, beauty, and fertility. For the Sumerians, she was Inanna; in Babylon, Ishtar; she was Aphrodite to the Greeks. All these goddesses were known for their beauty.

Venus in the world around us

She symbolizes art and music, the beauty industry (fashion, jewelry, and cosmetics), and gardens and the beautiful flowers that grow there. Venus signifies nature and its fruitfulness. She is represented by her signature color: green.

Rules **Taurus and Libra**
Day of the week **Friday**
Metal **Copper**
Color **Green**
Symbol ♀

ENJOYMENT | BEAUTY | COOPERATION | LOVE

ART & MUSIC | ROMANCE

RELATIONSHIPS | APPEARANCE | PLEASURE

VENUS

LOVE AND PLEASURE

VENUS **IN YOUR CHART**
The influence of this planet will be felt according to where it resides and its relationship to other planets.

BEAUTY Beauty is in the eye of the beholder. The placement of Venus in our chart tells us the kind of people we are drawn to; in art, it refers to what pleases the eye.

VALUES Venus reflects what we care about in life. It shows our tastes—our likes and dislikes. In Venus, we find the types of things and choices that make us happy.

RELATIONSHIPS Here, we want to form bonds with others. We can look to this planet to describe all kinds of one-to-one relationships, including friendships.

PEACEMAKER Venus is a peacemaker: she brings harmony, proportion, and balance to life (sadly, also a potential for laziness). You avoid conflict where Venus is in your chart.

VENUS **THROUGH THE SIGNS**

Consider how this planet expresses itself according to the sign that it occupies.

Aries You love the chase! You probably don't wait to be invited out with friends. You'll make the first move.

Taurus This Venus enjoys the pleasures of the senses–a sweet-smelling perfume or beautiful flowers.

Gemini Communication in relationships is key. The art of conversation is important to you.

Cancer This area is high in sentiment and feeling; emotional bonds are strong. Your friend group might feel like family.

Leo You may be someone who loves luxury. You probably dress to impress and buy the best quality you can.

Virgo You show love to those you care about through simple acts of consideration and kindness.

Libra You no doubt have a great deal of charm. Your politeness and gracefulness win people over.

Scorpio For you, relationships mean a lot. When you care about someone, you care deeply. Trust is all-important.

Sagittarius You may be a free spirit. You want to spread your wings. Travel and new ideas fire your imagination.

Capricorn Your sense of beauty favors structure and definition–in a face, as well as in clothes or artwork.

Aquarius Venus here means you value your space and might see love as friendship. Your style may be unusual.

Pisces You are highly devoted to loved ones and have a romantic soul. You can be transported by music.

MARS

ASSERTION AND ACTION

Mars gives us the energy that makes us take action and allows us to follow our ambitions. Learning about your Martial style can be key to feeling full of energy and fighting fit.

Mars in the sky

When it is close to the Earth, Mars appears bright red. This is why it is known as the "red planet." This comes from a concentration of iron oxide (rust), spread over the planet's surface by violent dust storms.

Mars in myth

Greek Ares was the god of war and violence. His Roman equal, Mars, however, was honored for his warrior spirit, courage, and skill in battle. His personality suggests a more disciplined form of this planet's energy.

Mars in the world around us

Mars is a symbol for conflict: wars, riots, the armed forces, and police. It also symbolizes people involved in more peaceable activities: surgeons, engineers, tool-makers, barbers, and butchers, along with their tools.

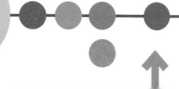

Rules **Aries and Scorpio**
Day of the week **Tuesday**
Metal **Iron**
Color **Red**
Symbol ♂

COMPETITION | SURVIVAL | STRENGTH | ACTION

COURAGE & DARING | ANGER

FIGHTING SPIRIT | ENERGY | CONFLICT

MARS

ASSERTION AND ACTION

MARS **IN YOUR CHART**

The influence of this planet will be felt according to where it resides and its relationship to other planets.

COMPETITION We might feel competitive in a number of ways–through debate or sports; as leaders or teachers; or in battles with family.

WARRIOR Mars symbolizes fighting spirit. When we feel threatened, it is Mars' influence in our chart that gives us the courage to defend our territory.

ENERGY Mars also indicates how we release physical energy through sports and exercise. Some prefer gentle activities, while others might like fast-paced action.

COURAGE Mars inspires us to be heroic and courageous. Our bravery might be physical, intellectual, or emotional. Mars may push you to "go the extra mile" to succeed.

MARS **THROUGH THE SIGNS**

Consider how this planet expresses itself according to the sign that it occupies.

Aries This is the most single-minded position for Mars. It suggests you have a strong, direct energy.

Taurus You only get angry when you've been provoked for a long time. You can also be persistent.

Gemini You use words as weapons. You feel liveliest when things are interesting and varied.

Cancer You are very protective of those you love. You tend to take a long, indirect route to get what you want.

Leo You are very heroic. You might take great pride in your athletic skills and lead the team.

Virgo You are practical and like to make and fix things. Exercise can help you feel better when you're angry.

Libra You use flattery and friendliness to win your battles. You might get angry when things seem unfair.

Scorpio You can cope with extreme circumstances. Anyone who crosses the line may get stung by the scorpion!

Sagittarius You have a need for adventure. You may love the outdoors or running.

Capricorn You focus your energy on quickly and effectively reaching goals you've set for yourself.

Aquarius A cool-headed Mars, you might find you act most effectively when you are defending others.

Pisces Under threat, you may disappear until trouble blows over. Still, you defend those who can't defend themselves.

"IF WE CANNOT **EXPRESS MARS**, HOW CAN WE **RESPECT** OTHER PEOPLE'S RIGHT TO **BE THEMSELVES**?"

Liz Greene and Howard Sasportas,
The Inner Planets: Building Blocks of Personal Reality

JUPITER

GROWTH AND OPPORTUNITY

The largest planet, Jupiter is named for the Roman king of the gods. The planet's vast storms reminded people of his thunderbolts. Jupiter is a lawmaker, but a charitable one. His other name, Jove, gives us the word "jovial."

Jupiter in the sky

Jupiter's circuit through the zodiac takes just under 12 years. The planet spends about 1 year in each sign. In keeping with the image of the well-fed authority figure, Jupiter bulges in the middle.

Jupiter in myth

The Roman god Jupiter was known as Zeus to the Greeks and Marduk to the Babylonians. These powerful gods ruled over their kingdoms with both kindness and harshness. This is why the astrological Jupiter is known as the lawmaker.

Jupiter in the world around us

Lawyers and legal systems, universities and colleges, religious organizations, publishing houses, and the gambling industry all fall under Jupiter's umbrella. A Jupiterian object might be a lottery ticket or a hot-air balloon.

Rules **Sagittarius; co-rules Pisces**
Day of the week **Thursday**
Metal **Tin**
Color **Purple**
Symbol ♃

GOOD FORTUNE | MORALS | PRINCIPLES

ZEST FOR LIFE | OPPORTUNITIES

ENTHUSIASM | ADVENTURE | HORIZONS

JUPITER

GROWTH AND OPPORTUNITY

JUPITER **IN YOUR CHART**
The influence of this planet will be felt according to where it resides and its relationship to other planets.

GOOD FORTUNE You may feel blessed with good luck: in friendships, athletics, family, academics, or other areas. Opportunity just seems to knock for you.

ADVENTURE Jupiter is your spirit of discovery–where you seek knowledge, wisdom, and meaning. Jupiter helps you when you create plans for the future.

CONFIDENCE Jupiter instills great self-assurance, which risks becoming arrogance. Jupiter is a dominating presence, so you may believe your way is the only way.

ETHICS Socially, this planet connects you to moral codes, rules, and laws. Jupiter shows you areas of your life where you have strong ethical principles and beliefs.

JUPITER **THROUGH THE SIGNS**

Consider how this planet expresses itself according to the sign that it occupies.

Aries With Jupiter in Aries, you are someone who can motivate others. You have a clear plan and can lead.

Taurus Abundance may be seen in practical terms–yummy food and a cozy home. Luck follows patience.

Gemini Your joy in learning shows an attraction to many subjects and varied knowledge. You may be a wordsmith.

Cancer Happiness comes from feeling safe in your group. You are often at the hub of the group, looking out for others.

Leo You have a flair for the grand and the extravagant. There is a warm and lavish side to you.

Virgo Good luck comes from paying attention to the details–and joy from hard work and developing your talents.

Libra You believe strongly in fairness, equality, and standing up for justice. You have strong social skills.

Scorpio You are passionate in your beliefs. This can make it hard for others to persuade you to see their point of view.

Sagittarius Jupiter here brings a sense of abundance and freedom. You are open-minded and want to try new things.

Capricorn This practical placement suggests being cautious when making plans. You believe in responsibility.

Aquarius You may want to pursue a wide range of interests. You draw energy from friends and community.

Pisces This suggests the escape from the daily grind. That can take the form of actual travel, fantasy, or spiritual practice.

SATURN

AUTHORITY AND MATURITY

In our chart, Saturn is serious and formal. It values traditions, limits, and rules. The astronomical image of Saturn is made up of clean lines, while the planet's rings suggest containment and restraint.

Saturn in the sky

In the ancient world, Saturn was the outermost planet visible to the naked eye. Until Uranus burst through, it formed the boundary of the universe. This position suggests its role in the chart as gatekeeper and authority.

Saturn in myth

After the fall of the sky god Uranus, his son Cronus (the Greek name for Saturn) took power. He established a Golden Age of peace and prosperity. In Saturn's role as beneficial authority, he encourages success through hard work.

Saturn in the world around us

Saturn governs thresholds and doorways, as well as government institutions. As a symbol of age and time, it signifies clocks and watches, rulers and measures. Anywhere cold, dark, lonely, or isolated comes under Saturn.

Rules **Capricorn; co-rules Aquarius**
Day of the week **Saturday**
Metal **Lead**
Colors **Black, gray, dark brown**
Symbol ♄

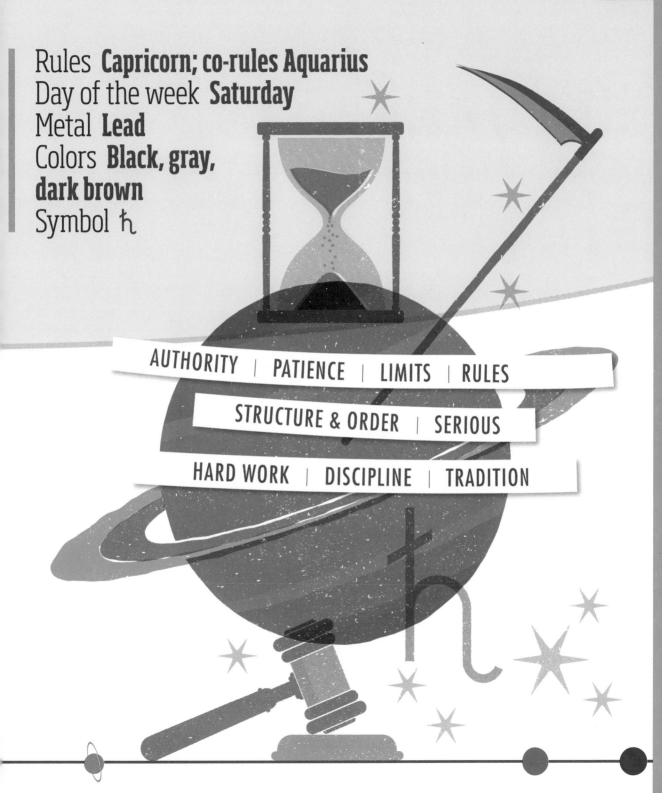

AUTHORITY | PATIENCE | LIMITS | RULES

STRUCTURE & ORDER | SERIOUS

HARD WORK | DISCIPLINE | TRADITION

SATURN

AUTHORITY AND MATURITY

SATURN **IN YOUR CHART**
The influence of this planet will be felt according to where it resides and its relationship to other planets.

SELF-CONTAINED Where Saturn is in your chart, you may want to focus your energies. You might find yourself working on solo projects, relying on your own abilities.

AUTHORITY Saturn is represented in authority figures: parents, teachers, and civic leaders. We see Saturn in police, judges, referees–those who set and enforce rules.

STRUCTURE Saturn brings structure, definition, and clarity to the world. It is where we can be organized, methodical, responsible, and committed.

BOUNDARIES Saturn shows us what is practical, realistic, and achievable in the real world. A sense of workable limitation helps us form realistic, achievable goals.

SATURN **THROUGH THE SIGNS**

Consider how this planet expresses itself according to the sign that it occupies.

Aries This suggests strong athletic or physical discipline. Saturn gives you the courage to achieve.

Taurus You likely possess tremendous patience, carefully following your goals until you reach them.

Gemini You may be interested in creative writing, learning a new language, or gaining technical skills.

Cancer This suggests a strong sense of duty and responsibility toward anyone (or anything) in your care.

Leo Although performance nerves can sometimes trip you up, you are proud of your creative pursuits and keep at them.

Virgo Care and precision are the gifts here. You might choose to develop expertise in a favorite subject or hobby.

Libra You are able to be a fair and impartial judge. You may be asked to weigh in during friendship disputes.

Scorpio Saturn can focus and control Scorpio's passion. This ability may make you able to weather trouble with calm.

Sagittarius You may be looking to learn more about religious traditions and your own spirituality.

Capricorn Duty and convention are important to you. Here, you are one to play by the rules.

Aquarius Your sense of social responsibility is strong. You may work for a cause you feel strongly about.

Pisces You are good at finding outlets for your imagination and poetic vision, perhaps in the arts.

URANUS

CHANGE AND LIBERATION

The discovery of Uranus in 1781 completely shattered the idea that the universe ends at Saturn. In our chart, Uranus represents the drive to be different and to cause change.

Uranus in the sky

Uranus is unique in that it is tilted at an unusual angle. Its polar axis lies horizontally, not vertically. This difference fits with Uranus's reputation as a rebel. Slow-moving Uranus spends 7 years in a sign.

Uranus in myth

In Greek myth, Uranus was a sky god. He had many children with his wife, Gaia. Their offspring started as lightning sparks that fell to earth. Another important figure is Prometheus, who rebelled by stealing fire from the gods to give to humans.

Uranus in the world around us

The element Uranium is an unstable, radioactive metal that eventually turns to lead. Like the metal, this sign shows that what begins as a new world will at some point become ordinary. The cycle will then repeat itself.

Rules **Co-rules Aquarius**
Day of the week **No allotted day**
Metal **Uranium**
Color **Electric blue**
Symbol ♅

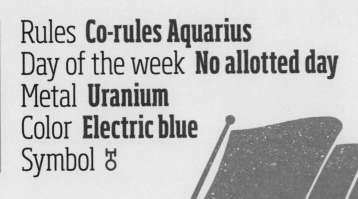

RADICAL | INDEPENDENT | INNOVATION |

UNCONVENTIONAL | REBELLIOUS

INTELLECT | ORIGINALITY | FREEDOM

URANUS

CHANGE AND LIBERATION

URANUS **IN YOUR CHART**
The influence of this planet will be felt according to where it resides and its relationship to other planets.

CHANGE You may look to Uranus to describe big changes in your life, good and bad. Where it falls in your chart, Uranus can bring excitement, but also uncertainty.

INTELLECT Here we are clear thinking, applying cool logic and scientific reason. Uranian ideas are often ahead of their time—bright sparks that light the way.

INNOVATION Uranus inspires us to be original. We may be free spirits, artsy, and able to solve problems in unusual ways. Be careful not to pursue change for its own sake.

REBEL Our independent style sets us apart from the crowd. We may be the outsiders, following a nontraditional path. Some are considered rule-breakers.

URANUS **THROUGH THE SIGNS**

As a transpersonal planet, the sign placement affects the group, not just the individual.

Aries *1927/8-1934/5 and 2010-2018/9* Technology advances. The car offers personal freedom.

Taurus *1934/5-1941/2* The Great Depression brings financial instability and changes in farming methods.

Gemini *1941/2-1948/9* The invention of radar revolutionizes communication. Borders change throughout the world.

Cancer *1948/9-1955/6* Family life and communities evolve to absorb changes brought about by World War II.

Leo *1955/6-1961/2* Television revolutionizes leisure time. The "Beat" generation shocks with new ideas.

Virgo *1961/2-1968/9* Innovations in health care bring social change. The silicon chip revolutionizes work life.

Libra *1968/9-1974/5* Equality of the sexes becomes an issue. Thousands gather for the Woodstock music festival.

Scorpio *1974/5-1981* The Punk movement captures the spirit of the age. People lose faith in government.

Sagittarius *1981-1988* Increase in air travel brings new freedom to explore the world. The internet is born.

Capricorn *1988-1995/6* Economic recession brings changes to professional institutions. The Berlin Wall falls.

Aquarius *1995/6-2003* Innovations in computing and communications (PCs and cell phones) create huge social change.

Pisces *2003-2010/11* The arts are transformed by technology, such as digital photography and CGI.

NEPTUNE

IMAGINATION AND TRANSCENDENCE

The blue-green planet Neptune is linked to bliss, loss, and longing. In our chart, it represents the desire to escape the real world into the limitless imagination.

Neptune in the sky

First sighted in 1795, Neptune had astronomers stumped; they weren't sure what it was. The planet was only officially discovered in 1846. It takes Nepture almost 165 years to orbit the Sun, which means that it takes 14 years to go through a sign.

Neptune in myth

God of the sea, Neptune is the Roman name for the Greek god Poseidon. A god of storms and chaos, he ruled over the ocean depths. The oceans symbolize the mysterious world of the collective unconscious, which is shared by all people.

Neptune in the world around us

Neptune can symbolize music, poetry, art, the film industry, photography, and fashion. Mystics and priests come under Neptune, along with hospitals, prisons, monasteries, and other places of retreat or group confinement.

Rules **Co-rules Pisces**
Day of the week
No allotted day
Metal **Neptunium**
Color **Sea green**
Symbol ♆

IDEALISM | ROMANCE | SACRIFICE | SPIRITUALISM

CHAOS & DISINTEGRATION | ESCAPE

IMAGINATION | DREAMS & FANTASIES

NEPTUNE

IMAGINATION AND TRANSCENDENCE

NEPTUNE **IN YOUR CHART**

The influence of this planet will be felt according to where it resides and its relationship to other planets.

SPIRITUAL ESCAPE Neptune is the part of us that wants to escape from ordinary life and find a higher purpose. A spiritual person might turn to prayer or meditation.

SACRIFICE Neptune brings out the charitable side of us that wants to give of ourselves. This may mean doing a kindness for a stranger or friend or working for a cause.

DISILLUSIONMENT We can become unhappy when reality does not live up to our dreams. People may let us down, but we hold on to our dreams.

CHAOS Neptune breaks down boundaries, which can cause confusion. The positive side of chaos is that it can fuel our imagination, one of our most precious resources.

NEPTUNE **THROUGH THE SIGNS**

As a transpersonal planet, the sign placement affects the group, not just the individual.

Aries 1861/2-1874/5 The art world is transforming; modern art begins. Religious practices are changing.

Taurus 1874/5-1888/9 Financial markets are unstable. Impressionist art focuses on natural use of light and color.

Gemini 1888/9-1901/2 Motion pictures bring a new form of storytelling. Post-Impressionism emerges in art.

Cancer 1901/2-1914/6 Curved forms inspire Art Nouveau. The old European and Asian empires break apart.

Leo 1914/16-1928/9 The "Roaring Twenties" and early films bring glamour. The Crash of 1929 ends the era.

Virgo 1928/9-1942/3 A loss of work and routine occurs as stock markets crash. The Great Depression takes hold.

Libra 1942/3-1955/7 There is a longing for peace after World War II. The ideal of social equality is seen in the US Fair Deal.

Scorpio 1955/6-1970 The musical revolution captures the 1960s. People search for transformative experiences.

Sagittarius 1970-1984 Interest grows in the West about spirituality and Eastern religions.

Capricorn 1984-1998 The Berlin Wall falls and Soviet Communism ends. Financial controls become looser.

Aquarius 1998-2011/2 Globalization leads to the rise of the "global village." Technology changes how we connect.

Pisces 2011/2-2025/6 There's no longer an absolute belief in science. People focus on stopping pollution.

PLUTO

POWER AND TRANSFORMATION

Demoted to a "dwarf planet" in 2006, Pluto remains a full "planet" in astrology. It is a symbol of deep human emotions. Pluto shows itself in our actions as depth, intensity, and transformation.

Pluto in the sky

Pluto takes 248 years to orbit the Sun and spends an average of 21 years in a sign. Its elliptical (oval-shaped) path brings it within the orbit of Neptune for part of its journey. At times, it spends 27 years in one sign and only 12 years in another.

Pluto in myth

The word Pluto comes from the Greek word *plouton*, meaning "wealth" or "riches." In Greek myth, Pluto is named Hades or Dis and is the shadowy god who rules over the dead. He is also in charge of the precious gems buried deep in the ground.

Pluto in the world around us

Pluto suggests the presence of hidden power or wealth: plutocrats, archaeologists, psychotherapists, miners, and underworld criminals. Spies, detectives, and secret service agents are happily embraced by this planet.

Rules **Co-rules Scorpio**
Day of the week
No allotted day
Metal **Plutonium**
Colors **Maroon,**
dark red
Symbol ♀

POWER | TRANSFORMATION | SECRETS | CONTROL

CYCLES OF BIRTH & DEATH | SURVIVAL

PROFOUND CHANGE | CRISIS

PLUTO

POWER AND TRANSFORMATION

PLUTO **IN YOUR CHART**

The influence of this planet will be felt according to where it resides and its relationship to other planets.

POWER Pluto gives us the strength to feel powerful; oddly, it can also show up at times when we feel powerless or invisible. At the end of the tunnel is the light of rebirth.

INTENSITY Pluto is like the planet, heavy and dark. This may come out as strong emotions. Practically, we may care about waste and recycling: giving trash new life.

SECRETS Pluto signifies the things we want to hide or that live in the shadows. We may keep secrets because we are ashamed. Secrets are often found where Pluto is.

METAMORPHOSIS We can compare Pluto's journey to the metamorphosis of a caterpillar into a butterfly. Like the caterpillar, it is inevitable that we all change and grow.

PLUTO **THROUGH THE SIGNS**

As a transpersonal planet, the sign placement affects the group, not just the individual.

Aries 1822/3–1851/3 Pluto was last here in the Victorian Age, which saw great change. It reflects new beginnings.

Taurus 1851/3–1882/4 The US Civil War and Franco-Prussian War impact the economies of the US and Europe.

Gemini 1882/4–1913/4 The telephone and newspapers change communications. The car is invented.

Cancer 1913/4–1937/8 World War I brings great upheaval. Family life and the role of women in society change.

Leo 1937/9–1956/8 Dictators Hitler, Stalin, and Mussolini gain power. The "Me" generation of Baby Boomers is born.

Virgo 1956/8–1971/2 Drastic societal shifts take place. The environmental movement gets underway.

Libra 1971/2–1983/4 The political balance of power shifts. Cold War negotiations take place.

Scorpio 1983/4–1995 The AIDS epidemic has a far-reaching impact. Apartheid is abolished in South Africa.

Sagittarius 1995–2008 Corruption in religious institutions is exposed. Financial extravagance causes a crisis.

Capricorn 2008–2023/4 Banking crisis leads to economic collapse and world recession.

Aquarius 1777/8–1797/8 Discovery of Uranus in 1781 symbolizes an age of invention. Pluto enters Aquarius in 2024.

Pisces 1797/8–1822/3 The Romantic Period in the arts takes place. Pluto next enters Pisces in 2044.

CHIRON

HEALING AND COMPASSION

Chiron is hard to define: it has been called an asteroid, a comet, and a minor planet. In our chart, Chiron represents our desire to heal. It can point to times in our lives that we have been hurt, physically or emotionally.

Chiron in the sky

Discovered in 1977, Chiron is much smaller than the other astrological planets. Still, it has taken on outsized importance as a symbol of our times. It was described as a "maverick" by the astronomer who first plotted its path.

Chiron in myth

The centaur (half-man, half-horse) Chiron's parents were the nymph Philyra and Cronus. They both rejected him, so he was raised by Apollo, god of music, poetry, and healing. Chiron, too, became a wise prophet, healer, musician, and teacher.

Chiron in the world around us

Chiron is a relatively recent discovery and is not linked to many aspects in the everyday world. But we can certainly see Chiron's image reflected in the world of complementary medicine, alternative spirituality, and ecology.

Rules **None**
Day of the week
No allotted day
Metal **None**
Color **None**
Symbol ⚷

MAVERICK | COMPASSION | ALTERNATIVE

VULNERABILITY | SCAPEGOAT

ALIENATION | TEACHER | DISPLACEMENT

CHIRON

HEALING AND COMPASSION

CHIRON **IN YOUR CHART**
The influence of this planet will be felt according to where it resides and its relationship to other planets.

WOUNDED Chiron shows where you may have been hurt, personally or physically. It may reflect a past family problem. Avoid feeling guilt for things that are not your fault.

HEALING Through acceptance, we forgive ourselves and others. Chiron is where we learn to be healers. The nature of our own wound helps us develop wisdom in that area.

OUTSIDER Here, we can feel like outcasts and scapegoats. We may feel like we're on the ouside of life looking in, that we are the person who is different from others.

INDIVIDUALITY Where Chiron is in your chart, you walk your own path. You can learn to develop and share your individual point of view and perspective with others.

CHIRON **THROUGH THE SIGNS**

Consider how this planet expresses itself according to the sign that it occupies.

Aries You may find it challenging to put yourself forward or to be assertive. Independence helps bring healing.

Taurus You may have felt some lack of security in your life. This has led you to value and seek stability.

Gemini Whether you excel in school or not, you probably have a gift for language and communication.

Cancer You may have a feeling that you don't always belong. Perhaps you see yourself as an outsider.

Leo You may look for a way to shine. Uncovering your creativity can inspire others to find their creative courage, too.

Virgo You may try to achieve perfection but feel you fall short. Mental and physical health are tied together.

Libra Times you've been treated unfairly may have led you to stand up for those who face injustice.

Scorpio Lack of power could be a theme for you to look at. Find creative ways to work through deep feelings.

Sagittarius You may be restless and trying hard to define what is important to you and what you believe in.

Capricorn You accept responsibility. If you see yourself as an outsider, it likely colors how you view authority.

Aquarius A commitment to social equality might come from a situation where you did not feel accepted.

Pisces This may suggest a loss, illness, or sacrifice. You can develop a spiritual vision and assist others to do the same.

THE
HOUSES

THE 12 HOUSES

The 12 houses reveal the areas of your life that are the most important to you. Each house describes a part of your experience, such as family or school. Each planet occupies a house. A house can contain more than one planet. Here's how to locate and interpret the houses in your chart.

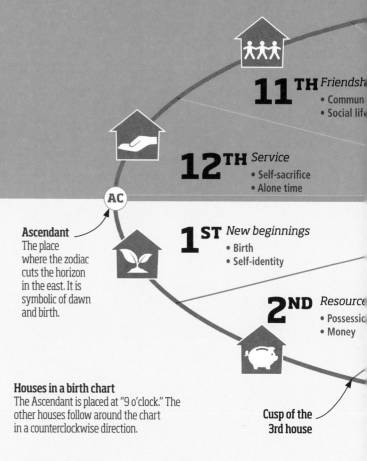

Ascendant
The place where the zodiac cuts the horizon in the east. It is symbolic of dawn and birth.

11TH *Friendsh*
* Commun
* Social lif

12TH *Service*
* Self-sacrifice
* Alone time

AC

1ST *New beginnings*
* Birth
* Self-identity

2ND *Resource*
* Possessio
* Money

Houses in a birth chart
The Ascendant is placed at "9 o'clock." The other houses follow around the chart in a counterclockwise direction.

Cusp of the 3rd house

> The houses represent **dimensions of the mind**, but also places of **everyday experience**.

HOW THEY WORK

The Ascendant, Descendant, MC, and IC form the four "angles" of a birth chart. One turn of the wheel equals one day in Earth's rotation. The planets hardly move in that time, but the angles and house cusps move like the hands of a clock. They create the picture of your chart. Except for the Moon, the planets for two people born the same day will have the same zodiac positions. Unless they were born at the same time and place, the house positions will vary.

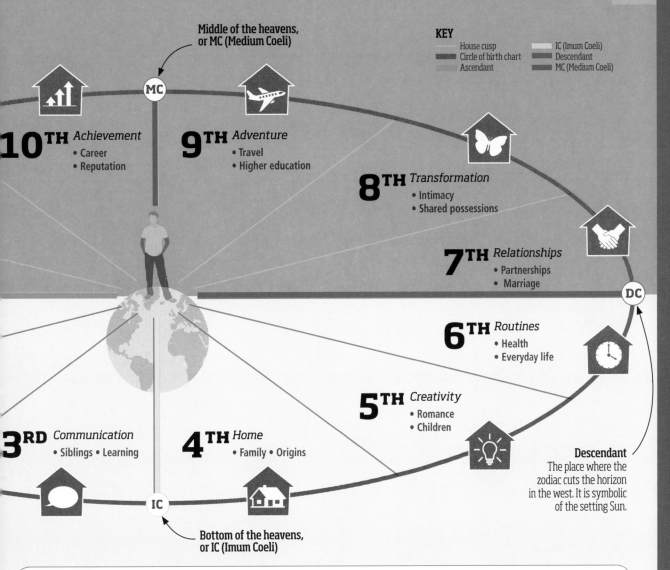

Middle of the heavens, or MC (Medium Coeli)

KEY
- House cusp
- Circle of birth chart
- Ascendant
- IC (Imum Coeli)
- Descendant
- MC (Medium Coeli)

MC

10TH *Achievement*
- Career
- Reputation

9TH *Adventure*
- Travel
- Higher education

8TH *Transformation*
- Intimacy
- Shared possessions

7TH *Relationships*
- Partnerships
- Marriage

DC

6TH *Routines*
- Health
- Everyday life

5TH *Creativity*
- Romance
- Children

3RD *Communication*
- Siblings • Learning

4TH *Home*
- Family • Origins

IC

Bottom of the heavens, or IC (Imum Coeli)

Descendant
The place where the zodiac cuts the horizon in the west. It is symbolic of the setting Sun.

» WHAT THE HOUSES MEAN

A planet in a house can be interpreted in two ways: from the perspective of the house or from that of the planet.

If you look at the house, the planet that occupies this house will impact your life experiences here. For example, with Mercury in the 1st house, for you to make your way in the world (1st), you will need to become a good communicator (Mercury).

With the planet, the house it occupies mirrors that planet's characteristics. With Mars in the 9th house, for instance, a way to develop a competitive edge (Mars) might be through adventure (9th house).

Most charts have a few empty houses. This doesn't mean these areas are meaningless. It simply means that your attention is naturally focused elsewhere.

1ST HOUSE

SELF AND PERSONALITY

The 1st house describes your birth and earliest life experiences. It also shows how you approach all new beginnings and the world in general.

First impressions

The 1st house symbolizes birth and new beginnings. It describes how we approach life and how our earliest experiences affect us. From a young age, this house shapes the way we see the world.

Appearance

The 1st house is like the display window in a store. Here, we create an image of how we want others to see us. This can be through our choice in clothes, or how we speak and present ourselves. These choices may be conscious, but they may not be.

Sense of identity

Planets in the 1st house have a big influence on us, and we identify strongly with them. If you have planets in this house, you are likely aware that they influence your personality. You may even be self-conscious about these traits.

The physical body

In astrology, the 1st house is closely linked with the physical body and its energy and strength. This house is important in influencing how you take care of your body and health and what you do to feed its vital energy.

PLANETS IN THIS HOUSE

Look at the planets in your 1st house to reveal how they affect your life. If you have lots of planets in this house, it will be a very important area for you.

The Sun You might have a strong sense of who you are. You work hard at self-improvement. Your father may be a powerful influence.

The Moon You do not hide your inner feelings. When making choices, you consider emotions. Your mother may be a powerful influence.

Mercury You are the one to start a conversation or create a connection. You are curious and eager to learn. A sibling could be a role model.

Venus Physical beauty might be important to you, and you always try to look good. You might see yourself as a peacemaker or referee.

Mars You probably came out fighting from the start and continue to do so. Your instinct is to take charge and show your strength and will.

Jupiter You are optimistic and see the chance to better yourself and improve your surroundings. People like your confidence.

Saturn When it comes to a new project, you like to be prepared. You have probably always been responsible. People come to you for advice.

Uranus You may not show your true self to others and may feel somewhat out of step. As an outsider, you can see different points of view.

Neptune Others may think of you as glamorous. Neptune gives you a sixth sense that helps you to be intuitive.

Pluto Naturally private, it is hard for you to open up. You may feel the need to be in control. You may go through many "chapters" in your life.

Chiron The wounded healer is strong here. You may experience loneliness at times, but it will make you sensitive to how others feel.

 SIGNS AND 1ST HOUSE PLANETS

Find out more detail by looking at which signs your 1st house falls in and particularly the sign at the edge of the 1st house in your chart.

Aries You are probably self-motivated and eager to get going–your own birth might be reflected in the way you take initiative.

Taurus You are slow to start, but steady once you do. Don't be rushed into action.

Gemini You need conversation and personal connection. You may feel like you're two people in one. A sibling may be a big influence on you.

Cancer Your first instinct might be to protect yourself. You can be territorial about people and places. Learn to trust your instincts.

Leo You are the one who takes action. You stand your ground if you feel pushed. You may have been encouraged to be playful and creative.

Virgo You have a gift for creating order and approach new tasks in an organized way. Physical health and nutrition may be interests.

Libra You move gracefully and dress with a sense of style. You like harmony and balance and are happiest in a peaceful atmosphere.

Scorpio Here, you may want to protect and defend yourself and others. You might take a warrior stance in life.

Sagittarius You may approach new projects and stages of your life with big plans. A change of scene can also bring a sense of renewal.

Capricorn You may be considered mature and reliable. Before you begin a task, you likely plan ahead and follow a tried-and-true method.

Aquarius Whatever might be going on inside, you usually maintain a cool exterior.

Pisces You may not have a good sense of physical direction, but you have imagination. Your subtle intuition can be a good guide.

2ND HOUSE

POSSESSIONS, MONEY, AND FINANCE

The 2nd is the house that determines our sense of financial and material security. The things we want to own and buy are shown here.

Money and income

The 2nd house denotes money, income, and the financial resources that we have. This house reflects our attitude toward money and the feelings it gives us. It shows what work we do and how we get money, as well as our spending habits.

Wealth

The "wealth" of the 2nd house is not just monetary wealth; it is all the other things that make our lives rich. If all our worldly goods were to disappear, what would remain? Health, love, friendship, joy in work and study enrich us, too.

Worth and value

We often use money as a way to describe worth and value. For this reason, this house reveals a deeper meaning. It shows our sense of what we hold dear. It tells us what we think is important and, ultimately, how we value ourselves.

Material possessions

The 2nd gives us a sense of "what is mine"—what you own and what you would like to own. Traditionally, it is the house of objects, possessions, and all the material goods we accumulate during our lives.

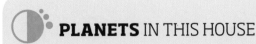 **PLANETS** IN THIS HOUSE

Look at the planets in your 2nd house to reveal how they affect your life. If you have lots of planets in this house, it will be a very important area for you.

⊙ **The Sun** Connecting to the material world or earning your own spending money might make you feel successful and creative.

☽ **The Moon** Emotional and material security are powerfully connected. Possessions have emotional significance. You like a nest egg.

☿ **Mercury** Communication skills can be an important resource. Treasured possessions might be books and other objects that value language.

♀ **Venus** You may like to be surrounded by beautiful objects. Material goods can give you pleasure.

♂ **Mars** You might possess an ambitious drive to improve your material conditions. You are proud when you earn money yourself.

♃ **Jupiter** You have a feeling of abundance and a confident attitude toward money. You can feel wealthy regardless of how much you own.

♄ **Saturn** You are careful with money. You likely don't expect to get something for nothing. You prize practical goods and self-sufficiency.

♅ **Uranus** Financial fortunes can rise and fall in life. You may experience a loss of money, perhaps by being careless.

♆ **Neptune** You may value giving more than getting money. Imagination and artistic gifts can be a source of self-worth.

♇ **Pluto** Material resources can be subject to change. Ups and downs in life will test your survival skills and create inner strength.

⚷ **Chiron** You may be sensitive to poverty in your community. You may volunteer or find ways to provide assistance to others.

 SIGNS AND 2ND HOUSE PLANETS

Find out more detail by looking at which signs your 2nd house falls in and particularly the sign at the edge of the 2nd house in your chart.

♈ **Aries** Planets in Aries here will take action to ensure security. You are likely self-motivated when it comes to handling your money.

♉ **Taurus** Taurus sits happily here, being associated with slow accumulation and the delights of material goods.

♊ **Gemini** Gemini brings a sense of light playfulness. Perhaps you don't take this area of your life too seriously.

♋ **Cancer** You may feel a need to guard your belongings and be possessive of things.

♌ **Leo** Material assets may bring you a sense of pride and self-worth. You may be a collector and value good quality.

♍ **Virgo** Thrift might have a big influence here. You know how to get "bang for your buck." You are likely good at keeping track of your spending.

♎ **Libra** Libra desires harmony, artistry, and good taste. This applies to your possessions, too.

♏ **Scorpio** Scorpio here can bring cycles of boom and bust. You learn from the changes. You are likely private when it comes to discussing money.

♐ **Sagittarius** You may prefer to make a splash and not count pennies. You need to be free to spend or donate as you please.

♑ **Capricorn** You show common sense and planning when it comes to money matters.

♒ **Aquarius** You believe in share and share alike and making sure everyone gets a piece of the pie. You value gifts of the intellect more than stuff.

♓ **Pisces** You are not always practical when it comes to money. You may have a tendency toward being overly generous.

3RD HOUSE

COMMUNICATION

In the 3rd house, we develop our communication style. Education belongs here, as do relationships to siblings, cousins, and friends.

Communication and language

The 3rd house is the territory of the mind. It indicates how we develop language and communication skills. Planets here show how perceptive you are and how you express your ideas.

Siblings

Through sibling relationships, we explore our world and flex our communication skills. Where we fit in the sibling tree–if we have older or younger siblings–can have an impact. Early life sets a pattern for how we will act in later life.

Short journeys and the local environment

Here, we interact with the immediate area around us. It influences how we connect to the community and travel through it. In contrast to the 9th house, this is the local world on our doorstep.

Early education

This house describes education and our approach to learning. When we begin school, we move from the secure family unit into the more complex world of school and classmates. Your planets in the 3rd house influence how you feel about this change.

PLANETS IN THIS HOUSE

Look at the planets in your 3rd house to reveal how they affect your life. If you have lots of planets in this house, it will be a very important area for you.

⊙ **The Sun** Language, communication, and the world of ideas lie at the heart of life. A sibling may be a role model.

☽ **The Moon** Learning may feel natural to you. You can absorb information easily and are highly perceptive.

☿ **Mercury** Your mind works quickly. You might play the joker in your group of friends or develop a role as a storyteller.

♀ **Venus** Here, you may enjoy romantic literature or exploring ideas around love and beauty. You seek harmony with friends and siblings.

♂ **Mars** Mars brings a competitive edge to your communication. At home, you might have to fight to be heard. For you, words have power.

♃ **Jupiter** You probably never run out of things to say and have lots of ideas. Foreign languages might appeal. You are an optimist.

♄ **Saturn** You approach learning seriously. Perhaps you help a sibling or friend with studies. You may have mastered a difficult subject.

♅ **Uranus** Your mind works at lightning speed. You can be single-minded in the way you think. Seeing all sides of an argument is your talent.

♆ **Neptune** You can be very perceptive and sense meaning without it being spelled out. The feelings conveyed in a story mean a lot.

♇ **Pluto** You may have a detective's mind, able to dig deep and find important information. You know that learning leads to personal growth.

⚷ **Chiron** You might have experienced nontraditional forms of learning. This may help you to see things differently than others do.

 SIGNS AND 3RD HOUSE PLANETS

Find out more detail by looking at which signs your 3rd house falls in and particularly the sign at the edge of the 3rd house in your chart.

♈ **Aries** Your mind moves fast, and you speak your thoughts directly. Perhaps there is some rivalry with a sibling or friend.

♉ **Taurus** You like to learn in a structured way and at a steady pace. You are drawn to practical knowledge–science and math, for instance..

♊ **Gemini** You might be good at noticing patterns, as well as making connections with people. You like to talk through your ideas.

♋ **Cancer** You may not be a big talker. You might like to communicate in writing instead.

♌ **Leo** You can be bold and confident in the way you express your thoughts. You are proud that you are good at public speaking.

♍ **Virgo** Whether it's your desk, room, or schoolwork, you like to be neat and organized. You might be a good observer and notice details.

♎ **Libra** You believe in fair and equal communication. You are naturally diplomatic.

♏ **Scorpio** You might enjoy research and diving deep into subjects that interest you.

♐ **Sagittarius** You may view education as a quest. You approach it with a spirit of adventure.

♑ **Capricorn** You might be a practical thinker. You can sort and organize information. You are not likely to waste time or put off tasks.

♒ **Aquarius** Perhaps you are part of a varied group of friends at school and feel like "one of the gang." You can be open-minded.

♓ **Pisces** You absorb information easily and do not respond well to rote learning. Books provide an escape into the imagination.

4TH HOUSE

HOME AND FAMILY

The 4th house describes your physical home as well as how and where you feel safe. It also describes how you feel about your family, ancestry, and history.

Home

The 4th house shows how we view "home." It is both a place of retreat and belonging and a physical house. The role your home fulfills can vary. It may be where you hang your hat or it could be where you go to recharge and feel secure.

Ancestry and history

Your sense of your family past, history, and cultural background are features of the 4th house. Connections to your country are part of this house. Here, we are also seen as guardians of the land and it is our job to care for the environment.

Family

The family we are born into and the family we make for ourselves are shown here. This house reflects a desire to belong. For those with personal planets in this house, a sense of being "from somewhere" might be important.

Foundations and private world

The 4th house is your place of safety within yourself. It is here that you can be your private self— what you are like when the front door is closed and you are no longer on show to the world.

PLANETS IN THIS HOUSE

Look at the planets in your 4th house to reveal how they affect your life. If you have lots of planets in this house, it will be a very important area for you.

⊙ **The Sun** Home is where you feel grounded and shine most brightly. You may feel a strong connection to your family history or culture.

☽ **The Moon** You might feel very close to your family. Being at home allows you to recharge your energy and feel emotionally secure.

☿ **Mercury** Your home might have a lively atmosphere. Perhaps you've moved house or had some change in your family life.

♀ **Venus** You might want a peaceful living space. Your family may be artistic or have a strong sense of culture.

♂ **Mars** There may be some competition in your home, perhaps with a sibling. Your own room can be a hive of activity.

♃ **Jupiter** You might feel like a traveler and imagining moving around lots or visiting different countries when you're older.

♄ **Saturn** You like to live in a stable, permanent home. You may be very responsible and look after younger siblings.

♅ **Uranus** You might be very independent. You imagine you won't stay in one place for too long when you're grown.

♆ **Neptune** You may search for the perfect sanctuary, a place where you feel safe and peaceful.

♇ **Pluto** Home can be your power base. You may want to redesign your home or move to a different place when you're older.

⚷ **Chiron** You may feel like you don't belong. It might take you a while to find a place that really feels like home.

⊛ SIGNS AND 4TH HOUSE PLANETS

Find out more detail by looking at which signs your 4th house falls in and particularly the sign at the edge of the 4th house in your chart.

♈ **Aries** There might be rivalry in your home, and you might have to stand your ground in the family group.

♉ **Taurus** Your home base needs to be solid and secure so you can slow down and take things at a more relaxed pace.

♊ **Gemini** You might have two homes or your parents might have very different historical or cultural backgrounds.

♋ **Cancer** You want your home to be like a cozy nest, a place where you feel really safe.

♌ **Leo** You are proud of your home and want to keep it looking nice. You might have lots of creative decorations in your room.

♍ **Virgo** You make sure you always straighten up before you rest. You might help look after your younger siblings.

♎ **Libra** You might be good at sharing and you probably hate it when situations are unfair.

♏ **Scorpio** You have a strong bond with your parents, but you also like to shut away the world and spend time on your own.

♐ **Sagittarius** You might come from a big, welcoming family. You might also have lots of visitors in your house.

♑ **Capricorn** You may like things in your home to be really well-organized.

♒ **Aquarius** You might like to live in a big community with lots of interesting friends around you.

♓ **Pisces** You might find a house by water or filled with music very peaceful. Maybe your family is very musical or artistic.

5TH HOUSE

CREATIVITY AND CHILDREN

The 5th house oversees creativity, play, and leisure. Activities here bring joy and make us feel special. Children come under this house.

Creativity and self-expression

Astrology places children in this house. Children have a great capacity for joyful expression, play, and creativity. The 5th speaks to the idea of making something lasting that shows our inner spirit and who we are.

Recreation

The 5th represents the child in everyone. Once we become adults, this part of people is often hidden from sight. It is important to take time out to smell the roses. Acts of fun, pure pleasure, and recreation nourish the life spirit at every age.

Romance

Planets here might indicate how we show love and how we make other people feel special. It also includes how we take care of ourselves. Romance is covered by this house. It includes the emotions we feel when we care deeply about someone.

Taking a gamble

Risk-taking in all its forms belongs here. That may mean literal gambling, taking a risk emotionally, or trying something new. With 5th-house activities, we often put our hearts on the line. It requires self-belief to see a project to the end.

PLANETS IN THIS HOUSE

Look at the planets in your 5th house to reveal how they affect your life. If you have lots of planets in this house, it will be a very important area for you.

The Sun You can be a natural performer or creative artist, happy to take the spotlight. You seek attention and praise.

The Moon You enjoy the world of play and are creative and fun-loving. You might want your personal needs to be put center stage.

Mercury Your creative talents may involve words and communication–as a good writer or storyteller. You want others to see you shine.

Venus You need to feel valued in relationships. You are a romantic at heart. Creative skills might involve design or fashion.

Mars You are competitive, and this shows when you're playing games or sports. As an adult, you will likely want children of your own.

Jupiter You might be part of a large family or group of friends. You enjoy making the most of recreation time. Play can be rejuvenating.

Saturn You could be good at strategic pastimes, such as chess. Creative work may include hands-on work, like sewing or pottery.

Uranus You have the potential for creative originality. The challenge may be to develop it. You need to follow through with one idea.

Neptune Music or poetry might appeal, and you may find it easy to lose yourself in artistic activities. These can bring spiritual fulfillment.

Pluto Your creative pursuits can be all-consuming and life-changing. They may give you a deep sense of power.

Chiron There may be adoption in your family history. Play turns out to be nurturing, both for you and for others.

 SIGNS AND 5TH HOUSE PLANETS

Find out more detail by looking at which signs your 5th house falls in and particularly the sign at the edge of the 5th house in your chart.

Aries Sports might need to be action-packed, a way for you to burn extra energy and get a thrill. Taking risks may come naturally to you.

Taurus Your creativity may be expressed in a practical way–for instance, working with your hands to make useful objects.

Gemini Your relationships may be a "meeting of the minds." You look for intellectual connections. Your creativity is likely to be verbal.

Cancer You may be a caretaker in your family or friend group, a role that makes you proud. A visit to the ocean or a quiet getaway energizes you.

Leo Leo here reinforces the power of creativity to give life joy and meaning. You are likely to be loving and warm-hearted.

Virgo You approach creative projects with care and precision, but you may have a tendency to hide your creative light.

Libra For you, a creative work must be beautiful and well-designed. You aim for perfection here. In people, you find classical beauty attractive.

Scorpio You may be loyal and passionate, but sometimes jealous. Your sense of humor is sharp.

Sagittarius Long-distance running or archery might be the kind of sport you would enjoy. You may dream of taking a vacation far away.

Capricorn You probably aren't much of a gambler. If you are, you take only minor risks.

Aquarius Being praised for what makes you different can make you feel special and valued.

Pisces You can lose yourself in relationships and not see clearly. You may see someone you care about through rose-colored glasses.

6TH HOUSE

HEALTH AND WELL-BEING

The 6th is the house of work and service. Here, we humble ourselves by doing necessary tasks and duties. These benefit the mind and body.

Daily work

In the 6th house, we encounter the day-to-day reality of work, whether that is schoolwork, housework, or a job. It shows how you can make the most of your experience. Your attitude toward work is also revealed here.

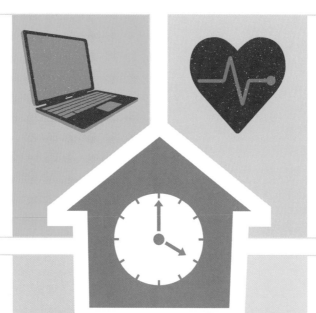

Health

The 6th house describes health as daily maintenance. Physical routines keep your body and mind working at their best. This house will also show how you might go about tending to your physical and mental well-being.

Routines and rituals

Rituals and routines give structure to our lives. Even though we may not always like everyday routines, they are essential to a contented life. Most of us would rather play than clean our rooms, but life becomes unmanageable if we neglect chores.

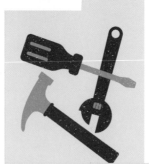

Service

In the 6th, we find our relationship to those who serve or work for us. It also describes how we serve others and what feelings this brings out in us. People who work in service industries might have planets in their 6th house.

PLANETS IN THIS HOUSE

Look at the planets in your 6th house to reveal how they affect your life. If you have lots of planets in this house, it will be a very important area for you.

⊙ **The Sun** You gain a sense of purpose by being productive. You may enjoy the sciences and have plans for a career in healthcare or service.

☽ **The Moon** You may be good at hosting get-togethers for friends. Hospitality work might appeal to you.

☿ **Mercury** Your particular craft might involve using your hands or learning a practical or technical skill.

♀ **Venus** You are likely popular among fellow students. You might be the one who unites a team. You need a peaceful work environment.

♂ **Mars** You feel liveliest when you work at your own fast pace. You may enjoy playing sports or getting regular daily exercise.

♃ **Jupiter** You get heavily involved in chores and gain satisfaction from a job well done. You may take on too much though.

♄ **Saturn** You can take your duties seriously. You might have a knack for fixing things. These skills could later influence your job choice.

♅ **Uranus** You probably need excitement in your daily routine. You may be someone who likes to set your own routine and timetable.

♆ **Neptune** Your skill might be to play a musical instrument. Daily practice is needed to develop your talents.

♇ **Pluto** You may leave chores until they feel overwhelming and then have to work overtime. Good nutrition helps keep you balanced.

⚷ **Chiron** You can be a compassionate mentor to others. You could be drawn to one of the healing professions later in life.

 SIGNS AND 6TH HOUSE PLANETS

Find out more detail by looking at which signs your 6th house falls in and particularly the sign at the edge of the 6th house in your chart.

♈ **Aries** You probably like an active daily routine. You push yourself to achieve a lot. You may be neat and tidy.

♉ **Taurus** A slow working pace might suit you best. This lets you complete tasks without too much pressure. Be mindful of your body's needs.

♊ **Gemini** You have a busy life and like variety. You can be curious about how gadgets work and like fixing things.

♋ **Cancer** Schoolmates might feel like family, and it is important for you to be emotionally in tune with them. Perhaps you take on a motherly role.

♌ **Leo** Because your sense of identity is linked to it, schoolwork takes priority. You make it shine by applying your own creative touch.

♍ **Virgo** You understand the value in everyday chores and are happy to do them.

♎ **Libra** You are polite and diplomatic with classmates and teachers. This approach helps you create the harmony you need.

♏ **Scorpio** Lots of activities or sports may be important to you. Remember to rest and recharge so you don't burn out.

♐ **Sagittarius** You may favor an independent way of working. You like a good-natured team.

♑ **Capricorn** It is important to you to complete a task well. You pay attention to details.

♒ **Aquarius** You may be drawn toward a technological or scientific field. You are a great believer in equality.

♓ **Pisces** Timekeeping might not be your strong point. Doing daily chores could bring some much-needed structure to your life.

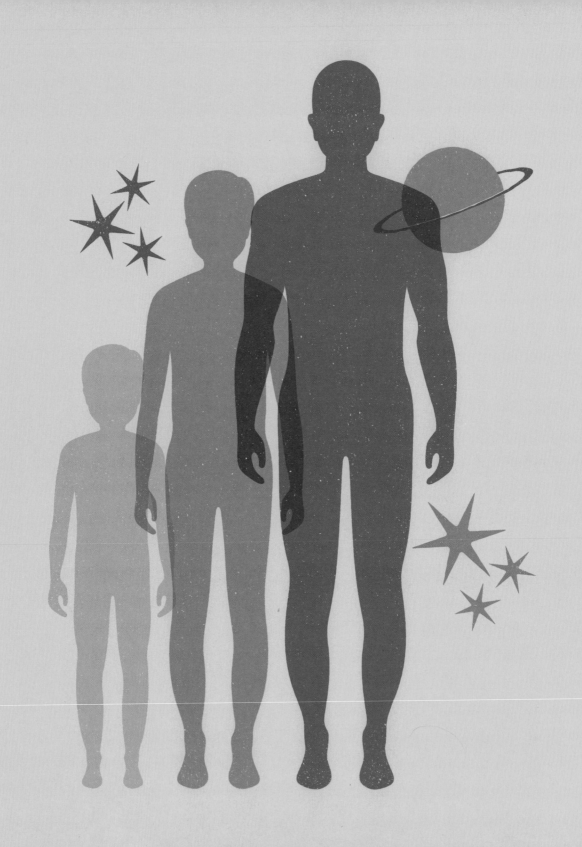

"[THE HOUSES] UNFOLD A PROCESS OF SUPREME SIGNIFICANCE– THE STORY OF THE **DEVELOPMENT OF A HUMAN BEING.**"

Howard Sasportas, The Twelve Houses

7TH HOUSE

RELATIONSHIPS

The 7th house traditionally has to do with partnerships and marriage. It also covers quarrels and disputes.

The other half

The 7th is our sense of "other." This can be described as a set of characteristics we are not aware we have and do not see as being part of us. We are attracted to whatever is in our 7th, sensing it to be a missing part of the picture.

Projection

Sometimes when we know a person, we see certain traits or behaviors as belonging to them. In reality, we may not realize that we have these characteristics. In psychology, this is called projection, and it is common in the 7th.

Relationships

This is the house of marriage and other contractual partnerships, such as partnerships in business. Later in life, if you decide to marry or choose to remain single, the sign on the Descendant and planets in the 7th will have a large part to play.

Open enemies

The 7th house is the "house of open enemies." It is here that disputes between two warring parties are settled. It is true that we can sometimes see partnership as a form of combat. The 7th is the place of lawsuits and the courts.

PLANETS IN THIS HOUSE

Look at the planets in your 7th house to reveal how they affect your life. If you have lots of planets in this house, it will be a very important area for you.

⊙ **The Sun** For you, relationships are at the heart of life. Make sure to find you own individuality and focus on yourself, too.

☽ **The Moon** You reach out to others in a spirit of caring. You are sensitive to feelings. You may look to nuture and to be cared for, too.

☿ **Mercury** You are attracted to smart people. You enjoy relationships where you can talk freely and discuss ideas.

♀ **Venus** Relationships for you are based on shared values. You will look for someone who is well-mannered and appreciates the arts.

♂ **Mars** Here, you may learn to assert yourself. Find balance. You should neither fight to be in charge nor let someone else take charge of you.

♃ **Jupiter** You are a good motivator and teacher, but may see others as knowing more. You may be attracted to different cultures.

♄ **Saturn** You want someone who is committed through good times and bad. It might take a while to develop your own inner authority.

♅ **Uranus** You may not want to be with someone who doesn't respect your freedom. Your need to maintain independence is strong.

♆ **Neptune** You may have a desire for perfection here. It might be hard for you to see people as they are, not as you would like them to be.

♇ **Pluto** Solid partnerships can help us change and improve. You may experience times of crisis that will teach you strength.

⚷ **Chiron** You can be compassionate and accepting of others. You may be motivated by a wish to heal.

 SIGNS AND 7TH HOUSE PLANETS

Find out more detail by looking at which signs your 7th house falls in and particularly the sign at the edge of the 7th house in your chart.

♈ **Aries** With Libra rising, you aim for fairness. You also develop a more warriorlike side that balances this.

♉ **Taurus** You look for stability and long-term loyalty in your interactions with others.

♊ **Gemini** You like to talk things out with people you are close to. You may need lots of variety and humor in any relationship.

♋ **Cancer** You may be sentimental about relationships. You might like to "nest." In the future, you may want to create your own family.

♌ **Leo** A secret desire for praise and attention could be at play here. Through relationships, you learn to show your specialness.

♍ **Virgo** You might look to others to provide some real-world foundation. With Pisces rising, you may get lost in daydreams.

♎ **Libra** Here, you must learn to compromise with friends and family. It may be frustrating, but you learn to be fair-minded.

♏ **Scorpio** You may be intense and passionate about relationships, even with Taurus rising here.

♐ **Sagittarius** Being with other people helps you to find meaning and develop as a person.

♑ **Capricorn** You look to friends and close relationships for a sense of stability and emotional support.

♒ **Aquarius** Relationships challenge you to develop a healthy give and take. You need to support freedom on both sides.

♓ **Pisces** You might use your practical skills to help others. You will likely find great happiness in relationships.

8TH HOUSE

INTIMACY AND SHARED POSSESSIONS

In the 8th, we encounter the darker side of life. Here, we can experience loss and crises. The 8th covers close relationships and finances.

Deep, dark, and mysterious

Death, loss, and compromise of power are all part of the 8th house. These challenge our sense of personal control. Much of what belongs here is deeply private and sparks universal and powerful emotions.

Shared resources

The 8th house describes shared money and belongings. This area can become a battleground if we are not careful. The 8th covers trust and mistrust. This is the house of debt and financial obligation.

Intimate relationships

After the contractual relationships of the 7th, the 8th house takes us into the territory of emotional bonds. In every relationship there are unspoken feelings. Power plays and deep knowledge are part of any close relationship.

Death and transformation

Here, we can experience renewal after a crisis or loss. In the 8th, we may encounter deep emotions from the past. We can learn and grow from difficult experiences. They can teach us to develop a strong inner strength.

PLANETS IN THIS HOUSE

Look at the planets in your 8th house to reveal how they affect your life. If you have lots of planets in this house, it will be a very important area for you.

The Sun Your life purpose might be to explore deep territories. You might do this through your work or personal relationships.

The Moon You can be very sensitive to the emotions others are feeling. You pick up what is not being said. You may be a caretaker.

Mercury You likely have a sharp mind and may be interested in research, coding, or other subjects that require intense concentration.

Venus You might like the power that comes with being in charge. You know how to be diplomatic and are good at negotiating.

Mars You know how to make up your mind and can take action and keep a clear head in a crisis. You have an independent will.

Jupiter You stay optimistic even in difficult situations. This trait allows you to be supportive of others. Faith may be important to you.

Saturn You may have a tendency to want to be in control. People trust you with their money and with their deepest secrets.

Uranus You tend to be a rational and practical person. It might be important to you to maintain your distance in relationships.

Neptune Giving your all in a close relationship can bring an emotional connection. It can also mean making sacrifices or feeling vulnerable.

Pluto You have a nose for personal power struggles and can play opponents at their own game.

Chiron You can understand others' pain and are likely to reach out in a spirit of compassion and healing.

 SIGNS AND 8TH HOUSE PLANETS

Find out more detail by looking at which signs your 8th house falls in and particularly the sign at the edge of the 8th house in your chart.

Aries You tend to charge headlong into deep waters, acting first and reflecting later. You might be quick to fall in love or take risks with money.

Taurus Your attitude toward money is to be safe and steady. You may later develop an eye for investing. You are sensible and grounded.

Gemini You are curious to learn about hidden motivations behind people's actions. You feel close to someone you connect with intellectually.

Cancer You might protect your private world closely and be in touch with your emotional side.

Leo You might have the Midas touch when it comes to money. Having control over your own money is important to you.

Virgo You may be someone who needs a lot of time to process experiences of crisis and catastrophe; you need to think them through.

Libra You want financial matters to be fair. You may like to go "Dutch treat," which means that each person pays their own way.

Scorpio When you care deeply for someone you are likely to give a lot of yourself.

Sagittarius You could be a risk-taker when it comes to finances. With relationships, you may see them as adventures.

Capricorn You prefer to keep your money for yourself. You might keep a similar boundary around your heart.

Aquarius You are a rational person, able to see the difference between reality and fantasy.

Pisces For you, close relationships and emotional ties can be a route to escaping the ordinary and finding more meaning.

9TH HOUSE

QUEST AND ADVENTURE

The 9th house is our sense of what lies beyond the horizon. It invites us to travel. It also covers education, philosophy, religion, and morals.

Search for meaning

The 9th house is concerned with exploring unfamiliar territory. The purpose of going into the unknown is to gain experience, wisdom, and greater understanding—of ourselves and of the world around us.

Teaching and higher education

In the 3rd, we learn the basics through early education. In the 9th, we study at a more in-depth level. Our planets here suggest how we deal with this more complex level of learning.

Philosophy, religion, and belief

Here, we seek answers to life's big questions. Philosophy, politics, and law are in the 9th. Religion and faith are covered. This is a house of principles and political ideals. We find the ethics and codes to live by.

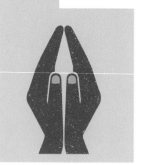

Adventure, travel, and long journeys

The 9th suggests long journeys. What you consider to be a "long journey" will depend on your perspective. It is not the mileage that counts, but your sense of something over the hills and far away.

PLANETS IN THIS HOUSE

Look at the planets in your 9th house to reveal how they affect your life. If you have lots of planets in this house, it will be a very important area for you.

The Sun Through travel or education, you can grow in confidence. At some point, you may need to move beyond the familiar territory of home.

The Moon The whole world can be your home. Perhaps you have lived overseas (or would like to one day). Maybe you have the travel bug.

Mercury This suggests a gift for languages, as well as curiosity for study. You are full of questions and interested in many subjects.

Venus Perhaps your purpose for study or travel is to develop artistic skills. Friends from other cultures might awaken this in you, too.

Mars You can be fearless about the unknown. You are the one to carve the path for others. Tough personal journeys test your strength.

Jupiter Faith may come easily, and you approach the unknown with trust. You always want to continue to learn and to teach.

Saturn "Fear of flying" might describe not just your feelings about airplanes, but also unfamiliar situations. You like to be prepared for any trip.

Uranus Going to college or learning about different religions can open your mind. You might be one to question values and faith.

Neptune The 9th is a house of the future. Spiritual vision and intuition are strong here. Travel might make you long for another place.

Pluto A few with Pluto here might be looking to be dominant. Most probably only want to grow and learn through study.

Chiron You may be likely to follow your own path. You will probably seek wisdom throughout life. You can help others on their life journey.

 SIGNS AND 9TH HOUSE PLANETS

Find out more detail by looking at which signs your 9th house falls in and particularly the sign at the edge of the 9th house in your chart.

Aries You want to explore and have adventures. You do not like to be held back. You might want to go to places that few have visited.

Taurus You like your physical comforts and don't like to rough it when you travel. You take a patient approach to learning.

Gemini Curiosity might be your main reason for study or travel. You are good at taking complex subjects and explaining them in simple terms.

Cancer Foreign cultures might interest you. You like to study subjects that you feel emotionally connected to.

Leo You travel in style. Getting out of familiar territory strengthens your sense of identity.

Virgo You deal with the unknown by checking the details and having a plan. You can be excellent at analyzing complex ideas.

Libra Your moral code is based on equality in relationships. You may want to study social sciences, art, fashion, or design.

Scorpio You might be drawn to philosophy to answer life's deep questions.

Sagittarius The world might seem like an exciting place to you. Called to adventure, you want to experience it all.

Capricorn You might take a practical and businesslike approach to learning and teaching.

Aquarius Moral principles for you might mean supporting what is best for the group rather than the individual.

Pisces You want to escape, perhaps not knowing what your destination is. Faraway lands inspire your imagination.

10TH HOUSE

CAREER AND CALLING

The 10th house describes our public image. It shapes what we do for a living and our role in the wider world. Here, we reach for success.

Career and vocation

The 10th house represents the idea of reaching a high point. It describes career and is where we aim for success and achievement. It is also the place where we find fulfillment through work. That work may be paid, volunteer, or family-based.

Parents and authority

The 10th house represents authority figures, particularly our parents. The way you take charge and lead will also be shown. Your style may be based on what you learned at home. This house helps us find leadership skills within ourselves.

Ambition and status

In the 10th house, we want to be rewarded for our achievements. We want to blossom and come into our own. This house serves us as we grow up and learn to achieve through work. Here, we take our place in the world.

Public image

The 10th is our public face, what we are known for. The profession we will eventually choose will show what matters to us. In the 10th, we seek work that is a happy marriage of worldly ambition and inner calling.

PLANETS IN THIS HOUSE

Look at the planets in your 10th house to reveal how they affect your life. If you have lots of planets in this house, it will be a very important area for you.

The Sun You will want to identify strongly with the work you do. You will be happiest choosing a job where you can play a central role.

The Moon You lead through a caring touch. You need to feel closely involved at work. Catering or home care may appeal.

Mercury Your career might revolve around communication and networking. You are drawn to talkative, clever people.

Venus You are probably good at bringing a team together. You always pay attention to how you look.

Mars You might choose a competitive profession where drive and ambition are required. You prefer to be the boss.

Jupiter Your career needs to offer the possibility to better yourself. Your parents might encourage you to aim high.

Saturn You are someone who will shoulder a lot of responsibility. Although it might be lonely at the top, it can give a sense of achievement.

Uranus You may have some trouble with authority. You might choose work that encourages your independent spirit.

Neptune A career in the arts might appeal, or something that allows you to use and develop your imagination.

Pluto Others might look to you as a natural leader. Inside, however, it may take you a while to feel comfortable with power.

Chiron A career in healthcare or teaching might be your goal. It may, however, take you a while to find your true direction, or calling.

SIGNS AND 10TH HOUSE PLANETS

Find out more detail by looking at which signs your 10th house falls in and particularly the sign at the edge of the 10th house in your chart.

Aries You are most likely to be a self-starter. You are eager to show what you can do and get ahead of the pack. You like to lead.

Taurus Slow and steady characterizes your work style. You might be someone who will want to stay in one job or field for a long time.

Gemini You are someone who likes variety and and has a range of interests. You may choose a career path that calls on multiple skills.

Cancer A job involving caretaking, such as healthcare or social work, might suit you. You might like being part of a professional family.

Leo You care about how others see you, and you want to put your best foot forward. Perhaps you believe in self-reliance.

Virgo You may like to make things and create order. Work involving a craft might appeal.

Libra You aspire to be seen as someone who is fair and doesn't take sides. You might want to be a mediator (resolve conflicts) in law or business.

Scorpio Determination will characterize your professional path. You may want to help change the world.

Sagittarius The world is your oyster. There might be an international or educational aspect to your work.

Capricorn You are organized and a planner. You prefer a traditional career with specific training.

Aquarius You are friendly and inclusive. You do best on a team working toward a common goal.

Pisces It may take you a while to find your career path if you have no clear sense of what you want.

11TH HOUSE

FRIENDSHIP AND COMMUNITY

The 11th house is where we find our place within the wider group, through friendships and social networks.

Friends and allies

If the 5th is the house of play, the 11th is the playground. We share space and time with others and create a social circle of friends and acquaintances. Here, we find our buddies and supporters, those whose actions benefit us.

Teamwork

The 11th covers our social circle. It also suggests all kinds of group endeavors—councils, committees, and clubs. It marks how we participate in and contribute to something larger than our individual concerns.

Hopes and wishes

The 11th reflects our hopes for the future and how strongly we believe that our future will be bright. It shapes our attitude toward making plans. It also shows what we can do to turn our dreams into reality.

Common good

The 11th says a good deal about our political views and social ideals. It indicates how we think society should be. It becomes clear how prepared we are to put aside personal glory for the good of the group.

PLANETS IN THIS HOUSE

Look at the planets in your 11th house to reveal how they affect your life. If you have lots of planets in this house, it will be a very important area for you.

The Sun You define yourself through your friendships and shine brightest when your actions help others.

The Moon You might be naturally outgoing, thriving on mutual support. Your role in the group may revolve around nurturing.

Mercury In a social setting, you may have excellent networking skills. Knowing who's who can help you get ahead.

Venus You very likely find a way to fit in with the crowd. You use charm, humor, and manners to make friends.

Mars You make your competitive spirit work for others. Mars here is a warrior for the community, perhaps fighting for social causes.

Jupiter Where Jupiter is, things often feel effortless. This planet's jovial spirit helps you get along in social groups.

Saturn This house can suggest a commitment to friendship. You may cultivate a few strong friendships that will stand the test of time.

Uranus Here, the question is how do you maintain your freedom and still remain loyal to the group.

Neptune You might believe in the motto of "one for all." You could be willing to put the needs of the community before your own.

Pluto You might form intense friendships or commit yourself to a political ideal. Both can make you feel powerful.

Chiron Chiron often keeps us from aiming high. Yet, in the 11th, you might develop a role as someone who brings a team together.

 SIGNS AND 11TH HOUSE PLANETS

Find out more detail by looking at which signs your 11th house falls in and particularly the sign at the edge of the 11th house in your chart.

Aries You are likely to be very independent. You can be a social pioneer, lead your friend group, or feel energized by a hectic social life.

Taurus You tend to look for loyalty from friends and give it in return. You value lasting, long-term friendships.

Gemini Gemini here suggests a need for a varied social schedule and a diverse friend group. You and your friends keep in touch a lot.

Cancer For you, friends might feel like family. You gravitate toward the safety of the tribe.

Leo This house provides an area for you to shine your light. You are likely to devote a lot of time and attention to friends.

Virgo For you, it is less important to stand out from the crowd than it is to make a useful contribution to the group.

Libra This sign brings a sense of fairness and harmony. You may find yourself being the mediator between friends.

Scorpio You don't take friendship lightly. Depth and passion may characterize your friendships.

Sagittarius You may find joy in meeting people from different cultural backgrounds.

Capricorn You may have a serious nature and a tendency to take control. You might play the role of elder, the mature one in your group.

Aquarius You believe it is important for each member of the team to be treated equally. You believe in doing what's best for all.

Pisces You are a sympathetic and sensitive friend. You may look to charity work to help your community.

12TH HOUSE

SERVICE AND SACRIFICE

The 12th suggests release, the final house before the cycle of the houses begins again. Here, we can experience sacrifice and devotion.

Behind the scenes

This is the house of "self-undoing." What this means is that we may not be able to see our own abilities. We need others to recognize our talents for us to believe they are real. This is also a house of escape and withdrawal.

Higher service

The notion of sacrifice sits in this house. It means simply "to make sacred." This perfectly describes the idea that whatever is given in a spirit of universal love, compassion, and charity is a true gift to the world.

Universal and collective

Traditional astrology places many institutions here. Hospitals, prisons, religious organizations are all included. In such places, it is easy for the sense of "I" to be replaced by the needs of the group. Planets here take on an otherworldly quality.

Finding meaning

Perhaps the ultimate meaning of the 12th house is the idea of transcendence. This means leaving the material world–the wheel of life–to be in a state of bliss and calm. Here, we connect with the universe.

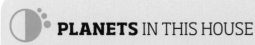 PLANETS IN THIS HOUSE

Look at the planets in your 12th house to reveal how they affect your life. If you have lots of planets in this house, it will be a very important area for you.

The Sun Your purpose may come from a life dedicated to service. You may also shine as a performer or actor, easily shifting into character.

The Moon Care work might appeal. Focusing your compassionate efforts in a small way can be more rewarding than trying to save the world.

Mercury You might be curious about the spiritual side of life. You may be interested in mythology, symbolism, and storytelling.

Venus Perfect romance probably does not exist, although you may wish for it. You may look for a reflection of your own beauty or gifts in others.

Mars You may be able to fight effectively and courageously on behalf of those who are weaker or less fortunate than you are.

Jupiter You may connect to the idea of having a guardian angel. You give generously and feel blessed with luck, too.

Saturn Knowing you are not responsible for the world's suffering can help you to make an impact where you can. You have a gift for organization.

Uranus Perhaps you hide your true self so you can fit in. Claiming who you are can help set you free. You may be a trend-setter.

Neptune You may give too much of yourself to others and to causes you're invested in. Sometimes this leaves nothing for yourself.

Pluto If you do not accept your own power (or feelings of powerlessness), you will not be able to reach your potential.

Chiron You are a compassionate person. You may have experienced some suffering, which makes you sensitive to others' pain.

SIGNS AND 12TH HOUSE PLANETS

Find out more detail by looking at which signs your 12th house falls in and particularly the sign at the edge of the 12th house in your chart.

Aries You bring your fighting spirit to help charities or causes you feel strongly about. You show initiative and focused energy.

Taurus You are drawn to nature. Time spent outdoors or in the countryside helps you recharge.

Gemini You may have a vivid imagination and a firm grasp of the concrete. You bridge both worlds.

Cancer You may be a natural nurse or caretaker. You may be the one who looks after the family pet, for instance. Home may be your sanctuary.

Leo You might feel your talents get overlooked. You can impress with your creative skills and gain confidence from the praise of the crowd.

Virgo You might serve through small, practical acts, for instance, helping with chores at home or listening to an upset friend. Such acts show love.

Libra Getting away from it all brings back balance. Perhaps you recharge by taking a long walk or retreat to a quiet place with a book.

Scorpio You might be cautious about the supernatural, but can have an intuitive sense of it. Mysteries or the mystical might interest you.

Sagittarius You may be a spiritual seeker. You may look for escape in physical travel, too.

Capricorn You can bring structure and purpose to work in an artistic area. Equally, you might distrust whatever you cannot see or prove.

Aquarius You might seek a scientific explanation for life's more mysterious aspects. Being with friends can be your escape.

Pisces You can be sensitive to feelings. You may become overwhelmed by the grief or sadness you pick up in others.

YOUR
BIRTH CHART

A PICTURE **OF YOU**

Your birth chart is a never-to-be-repeated arrangement of planets, signs, angles, houses, and aspects. It will help you express your individual spirit as you journey through life.

You are unique!

A birth chart is a view of the heavens at a precise time, date, and location. Each planet occupies a place in the zodiac, which is the same for anyone born at that time. But the location of birth matters, too. As time passes, so do the position of planets, angles, and houses. So, your chart is shared by no one else—not even a twin.

Your birth chart and you

A birth chart reveals your character, desires, and potential talents. It looks back at family history and forward to the future you will create.

Reading symbols

Each symbol has many meanings. For instance, Saturn can be about fear, but it is also about rising to challenges.

Time, date, location

To calculate a chart, you need your exact time, date, and place of birth. Modern birth certificates almost always record the time of birth, so that is the best place to check. If you do not know even an approximate time of birth, it is not possible to set up a full horoscope. You will only get a "flat" chart, which will miss a lot of basic information.

Casting a chart

To have your chart cast, you can consult an astrologer. They can either cast your chart by hand, or they will use special software to create it. There are also online websites that calculate charts for free. If you are new to astrology, astro.com and alabe.com are good resources.

An open mind

Be flexible in thinking about your chart. Be honest about challenges you face, but also honor skills you already have. A chart offers a picture of a life unfolding—one full of potential.

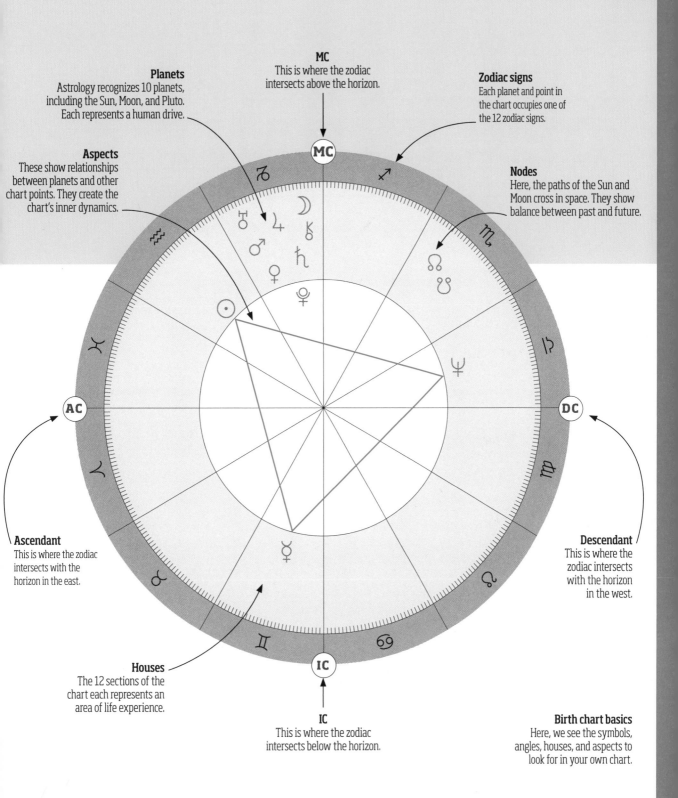

MC
This is where the zodiac
intersects above the horizon.

Planets
Astrology recognizes 10 planets,
including the Sun, Moon, and Pluto.
Each represents a human drive.

Zodiac signs
Each planet and point in
the chart occupies one of
the 12 zodiac signs.

Aspects
These show relationships
between planets and other
chart points. They create the
chart's inner dynamics.

Nodes
Here, the paths of the Sun and
Moon cross in space. They show
balance between past and future.

Ascendant
This is where the zodiac
intersects with the
horizon in the east.

Descendant
This is where the
zodiac intersects
with the horizon
in the west.

Houses
The 12 sections of the
chart each represents an
area of life experience.

IC
This is where the zodiac
intersects below the horizon.

Birth chart basics
Here, we see the symbols,
angles, houses, and aspects to
look for in your own chart.

THE **ASCENDANT -DESCENDANT**

The Ascendant and Descendant form an east-west axis across the birth chart. They link our conscious selves (the Ascendant) with our outside relationships (the Descendant).

Ascendant
The Ascendant sets the pattern for beginnings. The planet that rules your Ascendant is your chart ruler.

The Ascendant-Descendant axis
Here, we see how the Ascendant-Descendant axis cuts through the chart from east to west.

The Ascendant
The Ascendant (or rising sign) is symbolic of your birth. It shows what life was like at the time you were born.

New beginnings
This sets the pattern for birth and beginnings: how you come across when meeting new people, how you want others to see you, and how you fit into the outside world.

Persona
The Ascendant sign is our "persona," the person (sometimes the mask) we show to the outside. All our experiences are filtered through it. The Ascendant shapes our outlook on life.

The chart ruler
This is the planetary ruler of the Ascendant sign and it plays a key role. Your chart ruler does just what it says: it is in charge. Its position by sign, house, and aspects influences the story of your chart. Your chart ruler adds information to all the qualities the Ascendant describes.

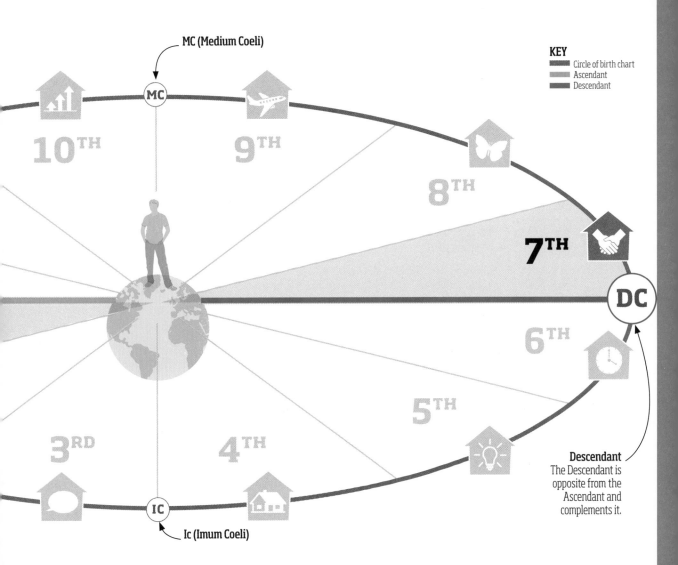

MC (Medium Coeli)

MC

KEY
Circle of birth chart
Ascendant
Descendant

10TH

9TH

8TH

7TH

DC

6TH

5TH

3RD

4TH

IC

Ic (Imum Coeli)

Descendant
The Descendant is
opposite from the
Ascendant and
complements it.

The Descendant
This is the point exactly
opposite the Ascendant. The
two ends of the axis are linked
as one horizon stretching
across the chart.

"Not me"
If the Ascendant is "me," then
the Descendant is "not me." It
is a set of traits we do not see
in ourselves. You will often
be attracted to people who
possess the qualities of
your Descendant sign.

Relationships
The Descendant is the part of
you that interacts with others.
The Descendant describes
characteristics that we
thought belonged to others
but in reality belong to us.
They can also be traits we
need to bring out in ourselves.
Through relationships, we
slowly develop the qualities
of our Descendant sign.

THE **MC-IC**

This north-south axis connects the IC to the MC. The IC represents home, ancestry, and private space. The MC is our ambitions and goals. Together, they are like a tree: the IC is the roots and the MC is the fruitful treetop.

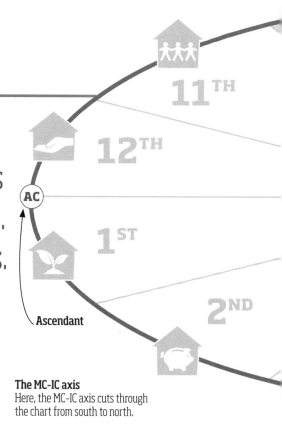

The MC-IC axis
Here, the MC-IC axis cuts through the chart from south to north.

The observer's meridian

If you can pinpoint the exact time and place of your birth, you can find your observer's meridian. This is where the north-south axis of your chart meets the east-west points above it in the heavens. The points where the meridian crosses the zodiac are called the MC (Medium Coeli) and the IC (Imum Coeli).

The MC

The Sun's daily highpoint is noon, which is why the MC represents high points in our lives. In the sign on the MC, we find qualities and activities we want to be known and admired for. This is our public profile. The MC also represents parents (particularly mothers) and authority figures who have helped shape who we are.

The IC

The tree image is a useful one for this axis. The IC forms the roots. It is the part of us connected to family, history, and home. It is what grounds us and also shows what has come before us. The IC traditionally represents parents (especially fathers) and their role in connecting us to family tradition.

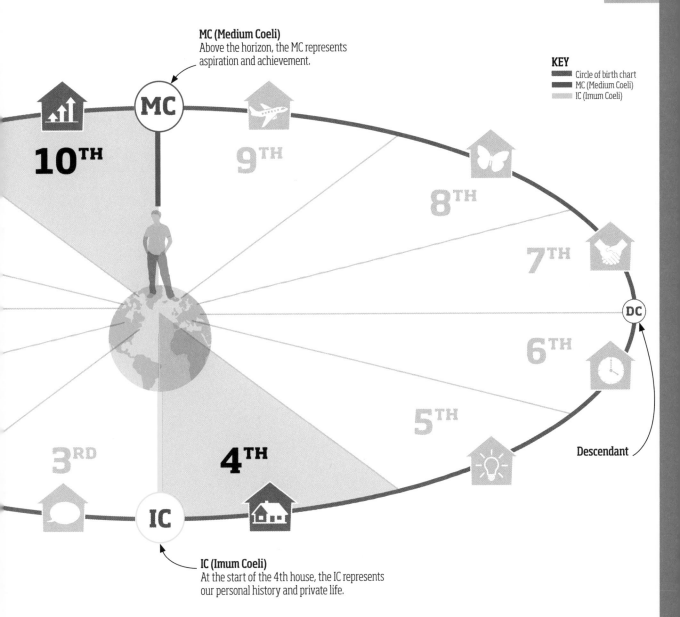

MC (Medium Coeli)
Above the horizon, the MC represents
aspiration and achievement.

KEY
Circle of birth chart
MC (Medium Coeli)
IC (Imum Coeli)

MC

10TH

9TH

8TH

7TH

DC

6TH

5TH

4TH

3RD

IC

Descendant

IC (Imum Coeli)
At the start of the 4th house, the IC represents
our personal history and private life.

" In the **sign on the MC**, we find
qualities for which we **want to be
known, admired**, and **respected**. "

THE **MOON'S NODES**

The North and South Nodes are the two points where the paths of the Sun and Moon cross. They are at opposite ends of the sky. In mythology, they are associated with the head and tail of a dragon.

In your birth chart

The Nodes form an axis where the two intersect, or cross paths. They are both powerful. At times, they work together, but they can also work against one another.

South Node Here, we find habits that may have been set early in life and reinforced over time. These may be a useful set of skills or negative patterns that we repeat because they are what we know. At the South Node, we learn to break habits that no longer serve us.

North Node The North Node represents unfamiliar territory. In life, we go back and forth between old habits and the unfamiliar. The two Nodes represent cycles of crisis, re-evaluation, release, and then forward motion. This pattern continues throughout life. The Nodes cycle around the chart every 18.6 years.

Moon at its lowest point

An astronomical view
Here, we see the path of the Sun, the Moon's orbit, and the line of the Nodes. When the Sun and Moon occupy the Nodes, solar and lunar eclipses occur.

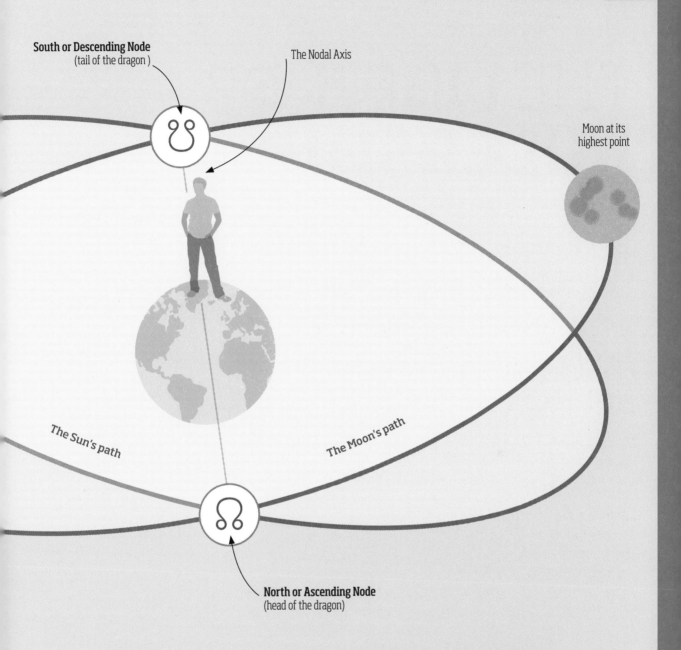

South or Descending Node
(tail of the dragon)

The Nodal Axis

Moon at its
highest point

The Sun's path

The Moon's path

North or Ascending Node
(head of the dragon)

> The Nodes represent cycles of **crisis**, **re-evaluation**, **release**, and then **forward motion**, a pattern that continues throughout life.

THE WHEEL OF
RULERSHIP

Each sign is ruled by a planet (or planets). Traditional astrology uses seven planets, from the Sun through Saturn. Modern astrology adds Uranus, Neptune, and Pluto.

In a birth chart

Everything in a chart occupies a zodiac sign. Each of your planets has a place in a sign. So do the four angles (the Ascendant, the Descendant, the MC, and the IC), the beginning point (cusp) of a house, and the Nodal Axis.

The zodiac sign occupied by a planet or angle tells us how they are expressed. The sign on a house cusp will cover the activities of that house. A sign modifies anything placed in it.

The planetary ruler of a sign shows us more about that planet, angle, or house cusp. For instance, for someone with the Sun in Capricorn, Saturn (ruler of Capricorn) gives information about what shapes that person's identity and goals. We can then look to Saturn's position in their chart–if it is in the 7th house, for example, then committed (Saturn) relationships (7th) will be at the heart of this person's life journey (Sun).

Planetary rulership
Here, we see which sign(s) each planet rules. The Sun rules Leo and the Moon rules Cancer. Each traditional planet rules the next two signs, working out toward Saturn. Chiron is left out.

“Everything in a chart occupies a **zodiac sign**. ”

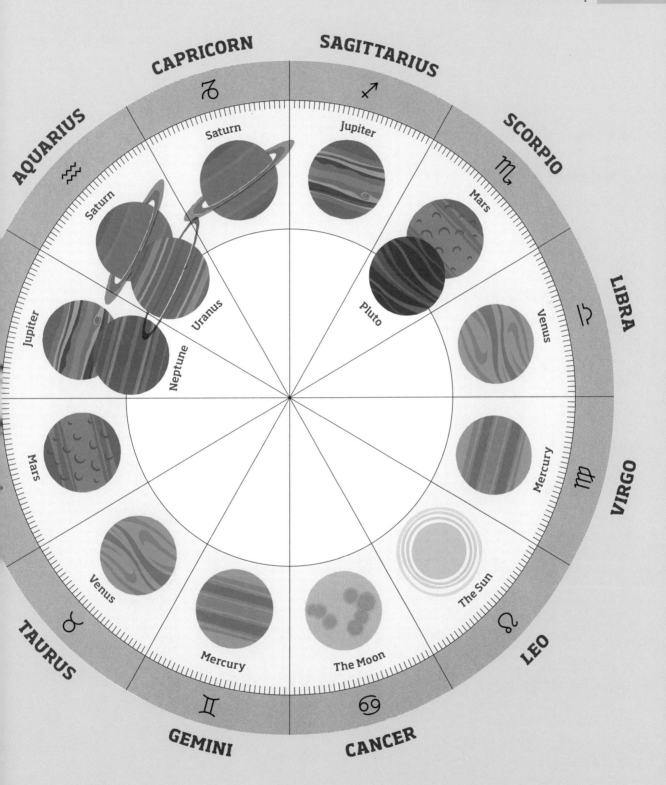

THE **ASPECTS**

Aspects are connections between the planets in a birth chart and between the planets and the angles or the Nodal Axis. They reflect our inner psychology.

Number system

Aspects are based on numbers and symbolism. They show the dynamics of the chart—how each planet really works.

Aspects based on 1, 2, 3, 4, and 6 are called major aspects. They form the main movement in a chart. Aspects based on 8 and 12 are minor aspects.

The opposition, square, semisquare, sesquiquadrate, semisextile, and quincunx are called hard aspects. Their numbers show tension. The trine and the sextile are soft. They are based around the number 3 and represent easy flow.

Each aspect has an "orb." This means that an aspect covers certain number degrees around a specific point. The tighter the orb, the more intensely we feel an aspect. Major aspects have larger orbs than minor aspects.

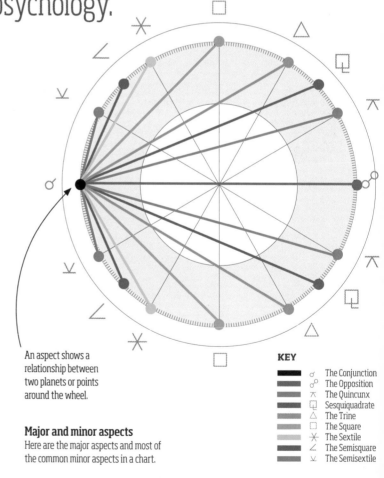

An aspect shows a relationship between two planets or points around the wheel.

Major and minor aspects
Here are the major aspects and most of the common minor aspects in a chart.

KEY

▬▬	♂	The Conjunction
▬▬	♂°	The Opposition
▬▬	⊼	The Quincunx
▬▬	⊡	Sesquiquadrate
▬▬	△	The Trine
▬▬	□	The Square
▬▬	✳	The Sextile
▬▬	∠	The Semisquare
▬▬	⊻	The Semisextile

MAJOR ASPECTS

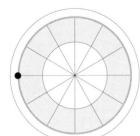

The Conjunction
Root **1** Symbol ☌ Angle **0°** Orb **8°**

Planets in conjunction are unified. They stay together and form a third energy.

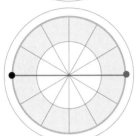

The Opposition
Root **2** Symbol ☍ Angle **180°** Orb **8°**

Conflict is reflected here. We may feel one emotion, but show another. Oppositions are about push and pull–things we want to bring together.

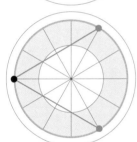

The Trine
Root **3** Symbol △ Angle **120°** Orb **8°**

The trine represents things we find easy and fun. We may take them for granted and not work to develop our talents in these areas.

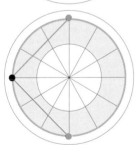

The Square
Root **4** Symbol □ Angle **90°** Orb **8°**

Planets in square are active. It may be hard to express ourselves, but we keep trying. Squares show connections to main themes in our lives.

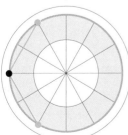

The Sextile
Root **6** Symbol ✳ Angle **60°** Orb **4°**

With sextiles, we are motivated, but also relaxed about expressing whatever is shown by them.

MINOR ASPECTS

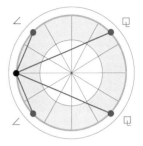

The Semisquare
Root **8** Symbol ∠ Angle **45°** Orb **2°**

The Sesquiquadrate
Root **8** Symbol ⊡ Angle **135°** Orb **2°**

These are similar to the square, but less intense. Here, we want concrete results and we set goals.

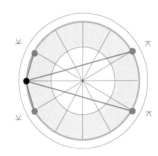

The Semisextile
Root **12** Symbol ⊻ Angle **30°** Orb **2°**

The Quincunx
Root **12** Symbol ⊼ Angle **150°** Orb **2°**

These aspects can frustrate us and be something we need to focus on to achieve.

READING A
BIRTH CHART

Before you interpret your birth chart, review the role each chart factor plays in building the whole picture of you. Here is an overview.

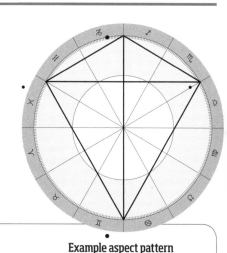

Example aspect pattern
Aspect patterns (see step 6) such as this kite will have a major influence.

STEP 1: **FIRST IMPRESSIONS**

A missing polarity, mode, or element will powerfully shape a person's character. Look, too, where planets are placed in the chart.

❯ Polarity/element/mode balance
Use just the seven personal and social planets (Sun through Saturn) and the Ascendant.

PERSONAL PLANETS					SOCIAL PLANETS	
☉	☽	☿	♀	♂	♃	♄
The Sun	The Moon	Mercury	Venus	Mars	Jupiter	Saturn

❯ Distribution of planets
This reveals basic traits about the personal and public self. Use all 10 planets, plus Chiron.

Upper half
The upper half is above the horizon. With most planets here, the focus is on the outside world.

East
A majority of planets in the eastern half suggests a focus on the self.

Lower half
The lower half is below the horizon. With most planets here, it suggests a more private life.

West
A majority of planets in the western half suggests a focus on relationships.

STEP 2: **THE ANGLES** AND **CHART RULER**

The Ascendant shows how you meet the world. Its ruler describes a territory vital to your life story.

The Descendant complements the Ascendant. The MC-IC shows the mix of private and public life. View angles separately, then each pair as an axis.

Take note of:

❯ **The Ascendant** (or rising) **sign**.
❯ **The Descendant sign** Contrast this with the Ascendant.
❯ **The chart ruler** Note which sign and house it occupies and its aspects to other planets. If Mercury, Venus, Mars, Jupiter, or Saturn are your chart ruler, check if it also rules another house.
❯ **The ruler of the Descendant** by sign, house, and aspect.

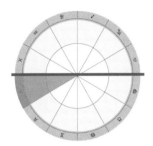

The Ascendant
Which sign sits on the eastern horizon of your chart?

The Descendant
Which sign sits on the western horizon of your chart?

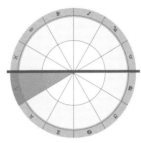

The chart ruler
Which sign and house does it occupy?

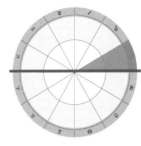

Descendant ruler
Which sign and house does it occupy?

Repeat this for **The MC-IC axis**

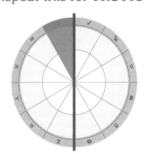

The MC
Which sign does the cusp of the 10th house occupy?

The IC
Which sign does the cusp of the 4th house occupy?

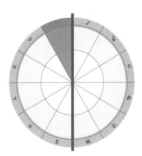

The MC ruler
Which sign and house does it occupy?

The IC ruler
Which sign and house does it occupy?

❯ **Planets and the angles**
Planets considered to be "angular planets" will strongly color your experience.

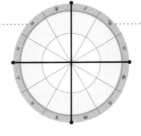

Angular planets
A planet within 8° of an angle.

CONTINUED

STEP 3: **THE SUN** AND **MOON**

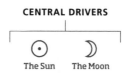

CENTRAL DRIVERS

The Sun   The Moon

With the chart ruler, the Sun and Moon are central. Review them by sign, house, and aspect. Check the house each one rules.

STEP 4: **THE PERSONAL** AND **SOCIAL PLANETS**

Explore the rest of the personal planets (Mercury, Venus, and Mars) to complete the core personality. Social planets (Jupiter and Saturn) suggest experiences of the wider world.

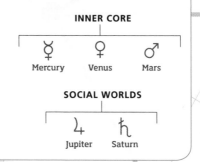

INNER CORE

Mercury   Venus   Mars

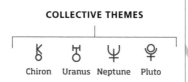

SOCIAL WORLDS

Jupiter   Saturn

STEP 5: **CHIRON** AND **THE OUTER PLANETS**

Chiron and the outer planets can be powerful, depending on their position. Note their sign, house position, and aspects, plus the house each rules.

COLLECTIVE THEMES

Chiron   Uranus   Neptune   Pluto

STEP 6: **ASPECT PATTERNS**

With an overview of each planet, the aspect patterns are easier to spot. Not all charts will have one.

STEP 7: **THE MOON'S NODES**

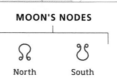

MOON'S NODES

North   South

The Nodal axis often makes more sense once we understand the rest of the chart and its themes.

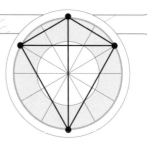

IDENTIFYING THEMES IN YOUR CHART

The goal is to pick out your chart's most important features. We are looking for clear themes, as well as the contradictions that all charts contain.

STEP 1: **IDENTIFYING THE KEY ASTROLOGICAL FACTORS**

The Ascendant, chart ruler, Sun, and Moon

These are the most important factors in any chart. They define your self-image and your worldview (Ascendant and chart ruler), your purpose (Sun), and your inner life (Moon). The houses they rule show key ways you express yourself.

Angular planets An angular planet will always play a leading role in your chart.

It will influence the house (or houses) that the planet rules. It covers the most basic areas of life: identity (Ascendant), relationships (Descendant), home and family (IC), and career or calling (MC).

Unaspected planets

An unaspected planet represents an inner drive that may be hard to connect to.

Aspect patterns Aspect patterns reflect a complex inner pattern.

Dominant or not Three or more planets in one element or mode will make that your dominant style. The lack of an element or mode is also felt.

Aspects with tight orbs

These are keenly felt. What "tight" means varies, however. An orb of 1° is tight for a square if our maximum orb is 8°. On the other hand, 1° is not tight if our maximum orb is just 2°.

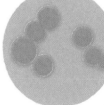

STEP 2: **IDENTIFYING THE MAIN THEMES**

A theme shows itself when two or three chart factors point in one direction. It is strongest when there are key factors from the list above.

Make sure, too, to look at a chart's strengths. Review the skills, talents, and challenges that you find in it. There is no such thing as a "good" or

"bad" chart. Each chart has difficult areas as well as points of positive potential. Sometimes, they are one and the same.

"BECOME WHAT YOU ARE!"

Dennis Elwell, Cosmic Loom:
The New Science of Astrology

GLOSSARY

Air signs Gemini, Libra, and Aquarius.

Angles The four angles are the Ascendant, Descendant, MC (Midheaven), and IC. They represent the four directions of the compass: the east-west horizon (the Ascendant-Descendant) and the north-south meridian (the IC-MC).

Aspect The angular relationship between two planets or factors in a chart. Astrology uses a set of aspects based on the division of the circle.

Aspect pattern A pattern of planets connected together. They create a particular dynamic based on the energies of the planets and aspects involved.

Cardinal signs Aries, Cancer, Libra, and Capricorn.

Cusp The boundary between two houses.

Cycle A full circuit of a planet around the zodiac. It can also describe a cycle as related to another planet (such as the lunar cycle).

Earth signs Taurus, Virgo, and Capricorn.

Elements The four elements are fire, earth, air, and water. Each zodiac sign is connected to one of the elements.

Ephemeris A listing of planetary positions each day at noon or at midnight. It also usually records information about lunar phases and eclipses.

Fire signs Aries, Leo, and Sagittarius.

Fixed signs Taurus, Leo, Scorpio, and Aquarius.

Geocentric Earth-centered. Astrology is a geocentric system, placing the chart's owner in the center looking out at the zodiac and planets around them.

Hemisphere One half of the chart, divided at either the Ascendant-Descendant axis or the MC-IC axis.

Horizon The horizontal line linking the Ascendant (in the east) and Descendant (in the west) across the chart.

Horoscope The birth chart. Originally, "horoscope" referred just to the Ascendant. Now, it refers to the whole chart.

House A one-twelfth division of the chart. A house represents an area of life, on both the physical and psychological levels.

House system The method used to divide a chart into the 12 houses. There are many different house systems. The most popular is Placidus. This is the system used in this book.

Lights The Sun and the Moon. Also known as the Luminaries.

Longitude Distance measured along the zodiac. On a birth chart, planetary positions are given in zodiac longitude–which means the position in the zodiac sign they occupy.

Luminaries The Sun and the Moon. Also known as the Lights.

Meridian The "observer's meridian" is a circle running through the north and south points of the horizon and directly overhead and underneath the observer.

Modes The three modes are cardinal, fixed, and mutable. Each zodiac sign is connected to one of the modes.

Mutable signs Gemini, Virgo, Sagittarius, and Pisces.

Natal Having to do with birth. The natal chart is the birth chart.

Negative signs The negative zodiac signs are the earth and water signs.

Nodes or Nodal Axis The crossing points of the paths of the Sun and Moon as seen from Earth.

Orb The space (in zodiac degrees) on either side of an exact aspect between two planets.

Placidus A house system. It is a method for dividing a birth chart into the 12 houses. Placidus divides the wheel by the time it takes Earth to turn on it axis.

Polarity The two polarities are positive and negative. Each zodiac sign is connected to one of the polarities.

Positive signs The positive zodiac signs are the fire and air signs.

Qualities An alternative name for the three modes.

Rulership Each planet "rules" one or two zodiac signs. The ruler of an angle or house is the planet ruling the sign occupied by the angle or house cusp.

Significator A chart factor signifies a desire, drive, emotion, or type of experience. For instance, Mercury is a significator for communication.

Singleton A planet that is alone in a particular polarity, mode, or element.

Table of houses A reference book astrologers use to calculate a birth chart by hand.

Transit The movement of a planet around the chart.

Water signs Cancer, Scorpio, and Pisces.

Zodiac The circle of symbols based on the 12 constellations that lie along the yearly path of the Sun.

INDEX

ABOUT THE AUTHOR

Carole Taylor, BA (Cantab), MA, FFAstrolS, is a full-time astrologer who combines teaching, writing, and client work. She is Director of Studies at the Faculty of Astrological Studies, where she was awarded a fellowship. Carole is co-author and co-editor of *Journey Through Astrology*. She is also a past editor of the journal of the Astrological Association of Great Britain and holds an MA in Myth, Cosmology, and the Sacred from Canterbury Christ Church University. She lives in West Sussex, England.

ABOUT THE CONSULTANT

Kim Farley, D.F.Astrol.S., is a tutor at the Faculty of Astrological Studies in London, teaching at Foundation and Diploma level. Kim has a particular enthusiasm for introducing astrology to beginners. Alongside her consultation work, which includes Children's Charts, she teaches private students and lectures for the London School of Astrology.

Publisher's Acknowledgments
DK would like to thank Kiron Gill for proofreading and editorial assistance.

Charts created using Solar Fire v. 9, published by Astrolabe, Inc., www.alabe.com

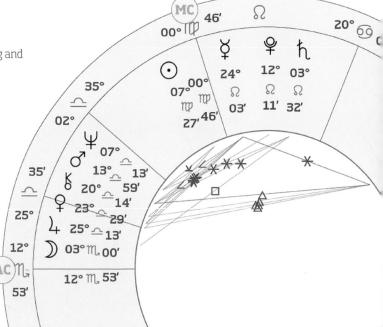